WOODCarving *magazine on*

THE
WOODCARVERS

WOODCARVING *magazine on*

THE
WOODCARVERS

GUILD OF MASTER CRAFTSMAN PUBLICATIONS LTD

This collection first published in 1997 by
Guild of Master Craftsman Publications Ltd,
Castle Place, 166 High Street, Lewes,
East Sussex BN7 1XU

© GMC Publications Ltd 1997

ISBN 1 86108 038 7

Printed and bound in Hong Kong by
Dai Nippon Printing Company

Front cover carving by Jonathan Fearnhead,
photographed by Dennis Bunn

Back cover photograph supplied by Peter Boex

Contents

Phoenix Rising 2
Ian Brennan (Issue 25, April 1996)

Large Scale Sculpture 6
Simon Latham (Issue 3, Spring 1993)

A Head Start 10
Ed Harrison (Issue 22, December 1995)

Lessons from the Landscape 12
Ted Vincent (Issue 25, April 1996)

Coach and Carver 17
Hugh Foster (Issue 8, March/April 1994)

The Enchanted Wood 20
Suzy Placet (Issue 20, October 1995)

Humorous Half Century 24
Roger Schroeder (Issue 28, July/August 1996)

Power Cuts 27
Alicia Beesley (Issue 26, May 1996)

Where There's a Will 32
Adam Styles (Issue 15, April 1995)

All Creatures Great and Small 35
Ann and Bob Phillips (Issue 28, July/August 1996)

Meeting the Challenge 38
Peter Pascoe (Issue 18, July/August 1995)

Finders Keepers 41
Stan Bullard (Issue 20, October 1995)

Only When I Laugh 46
Lori Freeze (Issue 21, November 1995)

As Good as Old 50
Roger Schroeder (Issue 27, June 1996)

Living Legacy 55
Benoi Deschênes (Issue 24, March 1996)

Personal Presentation 58
Zoë Gertner (issue 11, September/October 1994)

Land Marks 61
Robert Jakes (Issue 24, March 1996)

Big is Beautiful 64
Trevor Roberts (Issue 20, October 1995)

The Funny Furniture of Jake Cress 68
Harriet Hodges (Issue 2, Winter 1993)

Character Witness 71
Don Powell (Issue 17, June 1995)

A Public Debut 74
Richard Caink (Issue 19, September 1995)

Flights of Fancy 79
Judith Nicoll (Issue 25, April 1996)

Siberian Exile 84
Les Lee (Issue 9, May/June 1994)

Considering Carving 88
Ed Saylan (Issue 9, May/June 1994)

Mother Figures 92
Jackie McNamee (Issue 24, March 1996)

A Quizzical Look at Life 96
Tom Darby (Issue 5, September/October 1993)

Second Chances 98
Don Rankin (Issue 15, April 1995)

Ancient and Modern 102
Peter Boex (Issue 17, June 1995)

Lucky Strike 106
Mostyn Kimber (Issue 25, April 1996)

Street Style 110
Colin Wilbourn (Issue 16, May 1995)

Fresh Start 114
Ted Jackson (Issue 26, May 1996)

Victorian Venturer 117
Madeleine Wolf (Issue 25, April 1996)

Index 120

Notes

Please note that names, addresses, prices etc. were correct at the time the articles were originally published, but may since have changed.

Introduction

◆

When our forebears first shaped wood with a piece of stone or bone, they were starting a long tradition.

Since then, woodcarving has developed along with tool-making technologies. As new materials for tools became available, so they were adapted for woodcarving and in turn influenced the way wood was carved. Copper, bronze, iron and steel have all been adapted to carvers' requirements.

This evolution continues today with electric power tools. Specialist power tools have been developed for carvers, and other tools have been adapted. Powered gouges and chisels emulate the action of traditional manual tools, but other power tools are introducing new techniques.

Brave users of chainsaws employ the capacity for removing copious amounts of wood to create large scale works at great speed. For comparativley fine work, the Arbortech woodcarving disc and its imitators are used with angle grinders, to great effect. Flexible-shaft carving machines have been developed from dentists' drills. Used with small abrasive burrs, they can create detailed work finer than is easily done with hand tools.

Carvers now have a wider array of tools to choose from than ever before, opening new creative possibilities.

This book looks at the people who carve wood, and their work - carvers who are using part or all of the currently available range of tools. Some of those featured here have been carvers for the whole of their career. For others carving is a second career, or is running parallel to full or part-time jobs. Woodcarving is now more diverse than ever. A craft practised by a mix of people in a variety of ways.

There are physical education teachers, military chaplains, political exiles, cabinetmakers, college lecturers, teachers, chartered accountants, industrial modelmakers, plastics tool designers, students, policemen, tree surgeons, stonemasons, chartered engineers, general woodworkers, as well as artists and sculptors. Some came to carving in their youth, others in old age.

The articles in this book have been selected from the pages of *Woodcarving* magazine to illustrate the diversity of modern woodcarving, a craft that is still being commissioned for big houses, churches and monuments, but which is also used to decorate the houses and gardens of quite ordinary folk.

I hope the work in this book will astonish readers, and inspire them to find out more about the developing craft and art of woodcarving.

Neil Bell, Editorial Manager

I spend many hours
researching the subject,
using live studies
whenever possible

Left **Otters carved from
walnut and tulipwood
(*Dalbergia frutescens*)**
Right **Sleeping Lioness in
walnut, 24in 61cm high**
Opposite right **Bald
eagle with 8ft, 2.4m
wing span. The head
and tail were bleached**

PHOENIX

What a difference a decade can make. Ten years ago I was a cabinet-maker and, after many years of hard work, had built up a successful one-man business. I had more work than I could cope with and was soon to take over a larger workshop and a workforce to help with the ever increasing workload. Then disaster struck.

At 3.45 one May morning I was awakened by a heavy knocking on the front door. The police had come to tell me my workshop had been destroyed by fire. I immediately drove the few miles to see it for myself. I will never forget seeing the whole building which had burned completely to the ground. The large machines were glowing red hot in the darkness.

I lost all my machinery, tools, timber, a solid oak kitchen awaiting delivery and the remaining solid mahogany units I had made for the J class yacht Velsheda, which was due to take part in the Tall Ships Race.

Worse still, the workshop and contents had not been insured, as I had not been able to find an insurance company who would take on such an old timber building. Ironically my new workshop was insured, but empty.

Having lost everything, I wondered what to do next. With four months cabinet work in hand, I asked my customers if they would be patient and wait for me to reproduce their orders. They were magnificent, but when I had hired the necessary tools I could no longer afford to move into the new workshop. So I cleared some of the rubble and started again.

Career change

One day, scouring through the debris, I picked up a block of wood. It was badly charred on the outside, and my wife Suzanne said it looked like a dolphin. I had never carved anything in wood before, but in no time at all I finished it. My wife persuaded me to do a second one to see if the first was just a fluke.

It was my wife's chance remark which set me on a totally new career as a sculptor. A few months later I took a variety of carvings to a county show and had very encouraging results, so much so I decided to drop cabinet-making and concentrate on woodcarving.

It was tough going. I sold some of the carvings over the

RISING

After a fire devastated
Ian Brennan's first business,
a new career in carving rose
from the ashes

next two years and just survived. Being self-taught meant I had to learn by my mistakes, but as I have spent my whole life working on the premise of 'If all else fails, read the instructions', I was well equipped to cope.

No matter how good anybody's work may be, you need a lucky break. My first was when a casual visitor to a local zoo, where I was exhibiting work, invited me to put on a pre-Christmas show at the Freeland Gallery in Mayfair, London.

It was such a success the exhibition was extended for another six months. This encouraged me to complete my existing commissions and spend a year or two building up a large collection for a series of exhibitions.

After gambling everything we had, and making many sacrifices, I managed to build up a large and varied number of sculptures. They were mostly wildlife studies, some of which were life-size and included some bronzes. Things started to fall into place and venues were booked, the first of which was an extensive one man touring exhibition organised by the Hampshire Museum Service.

This ran for several months, closely followed by a series of exhibitions in galleries throughout the country, including

a number as Artist in Residence at the International Centre of Wildlife Art in Gloucester. As well as interest generated by the media, photographs and details of my work were sent by the Central Office of Information to embassies worldwide.

Crowns and coronets

Then a member of the Royal Household saw my work and was impressed by the standard of carving. I was approached to take on the commissions each year to carve all the crowns and crests for the newly appointed knights and members of the Royal Family, which are then placed in Henry VII Chapel in Westminster Abbey and St George's Chapel at Windsor Castle.

My first two commissions were the crown for the King of Spain and the crown for Queen Beatrix of the Netherlands. The work takes around two months each year to complete, and since 1989 I have completed 24 carvings, which have now been placed above the stalls in Windsor Castle and Westminster Abbey.

The latest is the coronet for Princess Anne, the Princess Royal, and Lord Kingston and Lord Ashburton Crests,

Left **Crests (18in, 46cm high) for Westminster Abbey before painting**
Below left **Painted crests now in Henry VII chapel in Westminster Abbey**
Below **A range of crowns and crests for Windsor Castle and Westminster Abbey**
Right **Work in progress on the scroll work for HMS Victory**

My wife's chance remark set me on a totally new career as a sculptor

installed in June last year. I have also worked on the carving for Sir Edmund Hillary and the Coronet for Lady Thatcher.

One of the many things I enjoy about these commissions is they are all different. They may range from crowns and coronets for royalty to carvings of animals and birds for Prime Ministers and other heads of state, or perhaps busts of men and women for the Armed Forces. They are all carved from lime (*Tilia vulgaris*) and then painted or gilded, maintaining a tradition first established in 1348.

Although I rarely do restoration work, occasionally interesting projects come up. I helped with the restoration work on Lord Nelson's flagship HMS Victory. This involved carving the intricate scroll work on the entrance port, being replaced on the middle gun deck.

Storm timber

My sculptures are made from a variety of woods, walnut (*Juglans spp*) and lime being my favourites. The terrible storms of 1987 and 1990 which hit Southern England provided me with a relatively cheap source of timber. I purchased for storage dozens of walnuts, limes and cedars (*Cedrus spp*) many of which were 150 years old.

Each sculpture is carved from a single piece of wood, so the huge trees being seasoned are important, especially in carving the life-size birds of prey I particularly enjoy.

When I plan a carving I spend many hours researching the subject, using live studies whenever possible, but also videos and books, until I have built up a complete picture in my mind of what the sculpture should look like. I have a natural ability to see things three dimensionally in wood which is extremely useful in this process.

Unless a client requests it, I don't make models or do sketches beforehand, or stick to a pre-conceived idea by drawing the outline on wood and then cutting it out. This technique would not help much working from a whole tree anyway.

I tend to work on the features of the sculpture as I go along, not only to try and give the sculpture a more flowing movement but also to give me the freedom to re-position the carving if a flaw in the wood suddenly appears.

Plucky project

A perfect example of this style of working was the life-size bald eagle in flight I carved in 1990. Although I had not attempted anything like this before and had little carving experience, a storm-felled tree gave me the opportunity to do something on this scale and I couldn't resist the challenge.

The tree was a 150 year old lime around 4ft, 1.2m across with a fork in it about 15ft, 4.6m from the base. Each of the two branches making up the fork were 2ft, 0.6m across and the eagle was carved from within the fork.

I didn't know what I was letting myself in for. To carve directly from a huge tree which was growing only a couple of

days before was bad enough. But the tree was also too heavy to move and had to be worked where it fell, on the side of a hill, in one of the coldest and windiest Januarys this century.

The conditions were just the start of the problems, and it was nearly five months before the work was completed. But I learned a lot from the exercise and it proved valuable for subsequent projects.

When I started carving the bald eagle I did not have a potential buyer for it, but it eventually found a good home in the Midlands. Although I enjoy working on large sculptures, the size can reduce the potential market. Most people would find it difficult to find room for them even if they could accommodate the cost of several month's work. But the contrast between working on a crown for a king, to a life-size eagle for an exhibition is what makes my work so enjoyable.

I have occasionally worked in bronze, but I much prefer the warm and living quality wood gives to the finished sculpture. The challenge of carving from a single piece of wood leaves no room for mistakes, and each one is totally unique.

The skills learned in my furniture days are sometimes put to good use. Earlier last year I was commissioned to make the Pascal candle-stand for St George's Chapel. Made from oak (*Quercus spp.*) and designed to suit the Medieval splendour of the chapel, it was completed in time for the Easter service and placed in front of the High Altar in Windsor Castle.

In the space of just a few years of losing my business, I discovered a totally new vocation and have achieved things of which I never realised I was capable. Fate has completely changed my life. ●

Ian Brennan is sculptor to the Most Noble and Honourable Order of the Garter and Bath. His work can be found in Windsor Castle and Westminster Abbey, company receptions and private collections all over the world.
He can be contacted for commissions at 21 Hornby Close, Warsash, Near Southampton, Hampshire SO31 9GN
Tel: 01489 574782

Simon Latham was born in London in 1964. He began carving wood on his Foundation course in Art and Design at Kingston Polytechnic. In 1987 he graduated from Oxford University's Ruskin School of Drawing and Fine Art where he specialised in sculpture. Since then he has been the resident artist at Plymouth College, Repton School and most recently Peterborough Cathedral.

Simon's work whether representational or abstract always derives from the human figure and is often concerned with a religious understanding of life.

Examples of his work can be seen in the grounds of St Anne's College, Oxford and Plymouth College, Plymouth in the Coronation Chapel St Katharine's Dock London, and Peterborough Cathedral.

Prince of Peace
1991 detail
8' 6" Sycamore
Peterborough
Cathedral

LARGE SCALE SCULPTURE

SIMON LATHAM

The carving of large pieces of wood presents a series of technical problems not least of which is transporting the raw material.

There is something uniquely satisfying about wood carving. I have worked with many other materials, but wood has a continuing attraction, it has a power and a life of its own which the carver can harness and direct. Sometimes a piece can be overworked to the extent that it is rendered lifeless, but more often, I trust, the dialogue between artist and material, the way we shape the wood and the wood shapes our ideas, reaches an interesting conclusion.

Scale

Until quite recently most of my carvings have been life-size figures. I wanted to make pieces which would confront people at their level, which would invade the space of the room and have a stronger more immediate impact than a smaller piece could. 'Prince of Peace' is the largest carving I have yet undertaken, at 8' 6" 2590mm, and here I felt that the larger than life scale was particularly important. In terms of scale at least, an adult becomes as a child before Him. His is a reassuringly strong yet gentle presence, 'the shadow of a mighty rock in a weary land'.

Scale is important, but working on a large scale does not, unfortunately, ensure a successful piece of work, rather it allows the possibility of a greater disappointment if the piece does not work out. I had a lot of trouble with the head of the 'Prince of Peace' and reworked it so often (each reworking necessarily resulting in a smaller head) that the neck became too long. Surgery was necessary and I removed a section of the neck with a hand saw and fixed the head back on with Cascamite and a couple of large dowels.

It was annoying to have to destroy the integrity

Prince of Peace 1991

of the trunk but the join is quite good and the problem resolved. As a rule however, I like to carve my sculptures out of a single continuous piece, so more often than not issues of scale are decided by the wood available.

**Prayer 1984
6' 2" Sweet
Chestnut**

**Stretching Youth
1992 13" Box**

Wood supply

It is, of course, possible to make a successful carving out of almost any piece of wood. I have used large tree trunks, firewood, old fence posts and processed timber depending on what I wanted and what was available. There is an enormous quantity of unwanted wood lying around England which can often be had for the asking. Farmers, land owners and private individuals have all supplied me with wood and have often given help with transport. Moving it can prove quite a problem and a large supply of willing and able-bodied friends are indispensable when it comes to loading and unloading tree trunks.

'I wanted to make pieces which would confront people at their level.'

An entire trunk poses the most problems as far as cracking is concerned, even if it has had a chance to dry. A trunk which has been halved or quartered will barely crack at all by comparison. For this job a chainsaw is usually required. My carving 'Prayer' is out of a halved section of sweet chestnut which helpfully split when it fell. The tree was in a park and my piece had been lying for about four months and proved very stable throughout the carving process.

'Prince of Peace' on the other hand, is out of an entire trunk of sycamore and has been subject to some cracking but not enough to disfigure it. In some ways the cracks contribute to the piece giving a feeling of antiquity and emphasising the flow of the wood. The cracking on my 'St Peter' is most distracting. The piece of oak was very wet when I began it and dried out rather too fast for its own good so the wood's natural infirmities were not helped.

Working methods

I usually 'sketch' out my ideas in small clay or Plasticine models. If I am making a large figure I will also do some drawings and measurements to ensure that the proportions will work out as

**Lord of the
Dance (iii) 1991
43" Cherry**

**Two as one, one
as two 1992
10" x 10" Yew**

required. I then transfer the measurements to the trunk and begin work with the chainsaw. It is helpful, in the case of a vertical piece, to up end the trunk when marking out, but I find it simpler and safer to do most of the chainsaw work with the trunk lying on the ground.

The chainsaw is an invaluable tool for roughing out a large carving. The only worry is of going too far too fast and making cuts that you afterwards regret. Some shaping can be done with the chainsaw alone, then by making a number of parallel cuts across the grain, say 4" 100mm apart, large chunks of wood can be removed quickly and efficiently with an axe or large gouge. Eventually the carving takes shape and the other gouges come into play. The nice thing about large carvings is that they stay still when you hit them and there is no fiddling about with clamps and vices.

Large gouges require a heavy mallet, mine is of lignum vitae, and correspondingly strong handles. The beech handles on my two largest gouges, a shallow 2" 50mm and deep 1" 25mm gouge, didn't last long. I found that boxwood handles stood up to the punishment quite well, but needed reinforcing with ferrules (I used thick copper piping). Last year however both tangs snapped within a week of each other; undeterred I exchanged my mallet for a lump hammer and a pair of ear defenders.

I leave a lot of my work with a chipped finish but have found the cylindrical and half round Surforms very effective. I do not like power sanders or drill attachments and end up using rasps and rifflers to remove the gouge marks. It is sometimes difficult to decide how to treat the surface of the completed carving. I would never varnish a piece, some I leave as they are, others I wax. A polished surface will emphasise the grain, but often a matt finish is desirable. I finished my 'Prince of Peace'

The trunk had been affected by rot so I thought it wise to take precautions; the resulting matt finish is very agreeable.

During my residency at Peterborough Cathedral I developed some large tubular figures in plaster. Since then I have been carving smaller pieces on a similar theme; smaller pieces do sell. After the initial roughing out no vice or clamp was of much use so I resorted to working the pieces on my lap, sometimes holding the wood between my knees other times in one hand, whittling I suppose. When nearing completion I put a rubber glove on my holding hand to prevent discolouration of the surface. It's a welcome change to take a matter of days rather than months to complete a carving but somehow the satisfaction is never quite the same when a chainsaw is not required to perform the overture! ∎

St. Peter 1992
6' 3" Oak
Peterborough
Cathedral

Learning to walk on water

Pamela Tudor-Craig talked to a young Christian sculptor about his work

Last Summer Peterborough Cathedral received the trunk and crown of the oldest oak tree on the Milton estate as a gift from Sir Steven and Lady Hastings. The gift has provided a young sculptor, Simon Latham, with the opportunity to create a major figure, a climax to his eight months as the cathedral's artist-in-residence.

Simon Latham had already displayed his statue of the *Prince of Peace* in the south transept. An exhibition, largely of his more abstract figures and drawings, was held in the Almoners Hall before Christmas. From the block of Cambridgeshire oak he was asked to carve a figure of St Peter, patron saint both of Peterborough and of its cathedral.

Mr Latham did his foundation year at Kingston Polytechnic and his degree at the Ruskin School of Drawing and Fine Art, Oxford. There followed years as resident artist at Plymouth College, and at Repton School, where he was also art master. From an artist with a background of this kind we might expect a scholarly work, well grounded in academic tradition — and we have it. Apparently he went straight into the block without preliminary drawings, and the anatomical proficiency of this very lively figure is praiseworthy.

The pose chosen is the opposite of the static form he had used for his *Prince of Peace*. St Peter is launching himself from the

side of the boat into the lake. Mr Latham did not want to show the old, bearded St Peter carrying his keys, but the clean-shaven and impetuous Peter whom Christ called from his nets. The features of this saint bear a striking but idealised resemblance to those of the sculptor himself — whose own face was the most willing sitter.

Simon Latham himself mentioned Michelangelo, specifically the *ignudi* of the Sistine Chapel ceiling, when he was talking about the influences on this figure; it was Michelangelo who resolved the problem of

conveying dynamic movement within the seated figure. Life, straining to escape from inertia, was the common theme running through Michelangelo's young men; and this is what Simon Latham wants to convey. His St Peter is letting go of the safe haven of the fishing boat to take the first risky step of faith.

The subject has been addressed very seldom by other artists. In the 1450s Conrad Witz painted Christ walking on the waters of Lake Geneva. There St Peter is floundering, arms outstretched towards his

rescuer as he has begun to sink. Tintoretto's *Christ Walking on the Waters* in the Kress Collection, Washington, has an already elderly and white-bearded St Peter putting a leg gingerly across the edge of the boat.

In both paintings the emphasis is upon the serene Christ, poised effortlessly over the waters. The saint plunging about near the fishing-boat is hardly more than a comic folly. But Simon Latham said he wanted to leave out the miraculous element, to concentrate on the metaphor of Peter attempting to walk on the water as a symbol of our own steps into the unknown. The material has offered a circle of patient tree rings around St Peter's foot, in a formation echoing that of a circle of ripples.

The phenomenon of walking on the water is not exclusive to Christianity. It is an attribute of Sufi mystics and Hindu avatars. It suggests an unusual harmony between ourselves and the natural world: the distinction between life in true harmony and the miraculous is a fine one. Simon Latham's figure is to be placed in the new walk at the east end of Peterborough Cathedral. His young St Peter takes a daring step into a new demonstration of man's more loving and reverent involvement with his surroundings.

Published by the kind permission of the *Church Times*. First published 10th April 1992.

The fifth of 16 children, I was brought up in the Ashdown Forest area. My mother and father met at Hastings Art School, and all of us have art in our blood. When I was eight I found some carving chisels in a box. I carved a cherub, and was hooked. These tools had belonged to my Great Aunt Constance, a very accomplished carver, who studied at Goldsmiths at the turn of the century.

Between the ages of 8-14, I became entranced by relief carving. When I was 13 I sold a marble of The Three Graces to a dealer in Greek art. After dropping out of Camberwell Art School, I married and in 1973 moved to Wales in a Romany wagon.

Together, we restored antiques, built pony traps, made wheels, furniture and anything in wood. It was only nine years ago that I found my own style, when carving an elm burr (*Ulmus spp*) head.

I had been asked to carve a smiling lion, but the wood seemed to tell me what to carve. The power of this piece fascinated me and a small burr mirror followed.

This also started as something else (a bowl) but the mirror came shining through and was finished in 40 hours. The rich deep burr carved beautifully and I enjoyed every minute of the work.

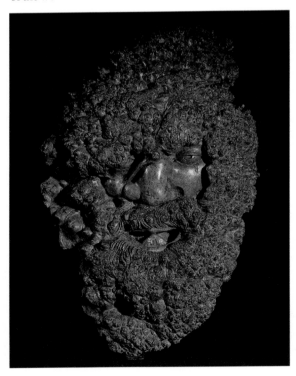

Ed Harrison carries on his family's artistic tradition as a carver

A HEADSTART

The rich deep burr carved beautifully and I enjoyed every minute of the work

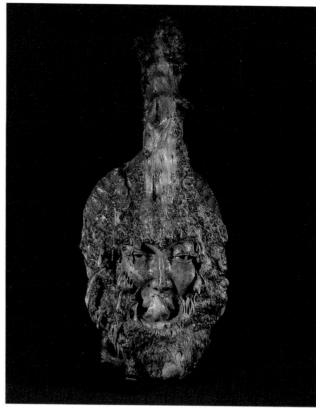

Opposite top
The Knight (from Chaucer's Canterbury Tales)
Opposite left
Elm burr head
Left
Small elm burr mirror
Above
Mask of Green Man. **When photographed the mask looks back at you**
Right
Large elm burr mirror

The mask of a green man was carved in a piece of yew (*Taxus baccata*) which had almost fossilised. You can only speculate how old the tree was. It had 4-5ft, 1.2-1.5m diameter hollow bowls growing from the same root. The three still growing were 27ft, 8.2m round.

I carved the large elm burr mirror at The Garden Festival of Wales. It illustrates clearly the detail possible with this type of wood. What a shame these trees have suffered so much.

I played with the idea of the yew and sycamore (*Acer pseudoplatanus*) mirror for the last five years, and I have just finished the mirror big enough to walk through.

Three years ago I helped to set up a carving event in Beechenhirst Park, in Coleford, together with the Forest of Dean, Forestry Commission, and another sculptor.

A great success, this event boasted seven sculptors and carvers last year. We had an exhibition, and the works were auctioned on completion. There was plenty for the children to see and do, many demonstrations and a sculpture trail.

This year's event, held in August, was also very interesting with eight carvers taking part from around the country. We each had a week to complete our carving and they all developed into very different pieces of work. The event is a lot of fun and we hope to have another one next year. ●

Far left *Pike with Boathouse* is 1m, 3½ft long
Left **This plaque to Blake's** *Hydraulic Ram* **is carved from a 1m, 3½ft solid piece and demonstrates Vincent's interest in this feat of engineering**
Below *Hydraulic Ram* is partly turned with carved leaves
Right **Column with Bullrushes** stands 8in, 20cm high

I have worked with wood for some time, and was given a Crafts Council grant to set up a workshop in 1980. I spent several years making limited batch production, decorative artefacts. Although based on similar themes to my current work, I gave no in-depth account of the subjects and, despite being hand-finished, incorporated shapes and forms which were often dictated by machine processes.

Recently, a two year period of research inspired by man's relationship with his surroundings, resulted in my exhibition *Echoes In the Landscape*. The show is composed of a sequence of words, pictures and objects. The small wooden carved and constructed objects, 30 in total, record and reflect the intense relationship between the ever-changing natural world and the equally transient manmade objects on its surface.

During my research, I spent as much time looking as I did making. I have always had a strong affinity with the landscape, a sense of place, treading the same footpaths, constantly rediscovering, peering into the same ponds, streams and rivers. Images I had carried with me for a long time gained clarity.

As I walked, I began to draw, photograph and measure fragments and objects, things with which I felt familiar. The more I looked, the more detailed and complex they became. Looking, seeing afresh, recording and understanding the world is an important part of my working process.

Natural engineering

I looked carefully at the relationship between living and inanimate objects, and at structures which follow the water on its course through lakes, ponds and rivers. The juxtaposition of the natural and the man-made gave me the idea of creating sharp contrasts in my work.

I took fragments from the water's edge, photographed them in context and remade them on a larger scale. They reminded me of the sensual quality of natural forms. I placed them in close proximity to interpretations of simple manmade structures, such as the drain cover we all know and tread on daily. Re-made in wood, they had an unfamiliar, yet inviting quality, making you see them anew.

Art joined closely with engineering in the form of industrial artefacts. The hydraulic ram, for instance, uses only the energy contained in the flowing stream and made me think of economy, from construction to consumption.

I observed other complex networks which use the power of water, and the man-made distribution system throughout the landscape. The hydrant, galvanised tank and water trough are commonplace objects in our everyday lives, which remind us of the presence of water and of our total dependence on its good management in the future.

From future hopes and uncertainties, I returned to the enigma of the stone column I had discovered in the sand of a millpond. Its beautiful carving depicted bulrushes and other

LESSONS FROM

FEATURE Ted Vincent explains how his work
explores man's relationship with nature

THE LANDSCAPE

water plants, a common theme throughout time. It had a hole through its middle, indicating the possible base of a fountain and made me wonder if a statue of Pan, which may have been seated on top, was buried under the sand and water.

Recreation in wood

I looked at all these things as a maker, the exact composition of the spiral in a snail shell, how many components made up a bird's skull and so on. I began to rebuild my observations in wood.

I used simple tools, gouges and chisels ranging from 1in, 25mm for larger pieces, down to ½in, 1mm for re-creating the delicate ripples of the water. I constantly re-established and re-worked the surface using scrapers and knives to get a fine finish. It was a steady, constant process of removing the wood gradually and methodically.

I tried to re-create different surfaces such as water, bone, shell, landscape, masonry and steel. I wanted to represent accurately the form and substance I was working from, heightening an awareness of its presence by changing its material and scale.

Educational artefacts

In my research and my work as a teacher, one of my concerns was to provide a stimulus through my work, to help individuals understand their position in relationship to their surroundings, both historically and in a contemporary context.

I was trying to give some insight to change, and working with others. I wanted to bridge the millennia, and bring the past and present closer together.

In my experience, a true understanding of these matters comes initially through first hand experience, the studies previously described, and by studying the work of others.

The British Museum, Museum of Mankind and the Victoria and Albert Museum were useful for viewing and understanding how and why others have produced artefacts in the past.

As the students looked and recorded, so did I. Here I could observe first hand, classical proportions, folk art, functional objects, applied decoration, the work of artists, craftsmen and tradesmen.

They all demonstrated a deep understanding of materials and processes, worked with great skill and with a relevance and meaning appropriate to their time.

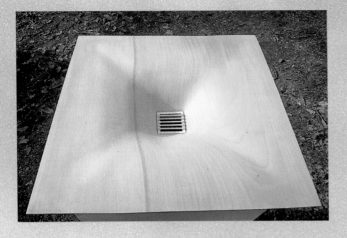

I felt a particular affinity towards objects which, as well as having a formal complexity, incorporated a narrative in their structure through some sort of surface embellishment.

An Eygptian wooden cosmetics' box, beautifully carved in the shape of a duck, medieval architectural post carving, 5,000 year old ritual objects from Skara Brae, were all small items which had been part of people's lives.

These careful, yet modest artefacts spoke with a directness which reminded me of the importance of human skills and the timelessness of the artefacts produced. They informed me further about my interests in fragments of my own time.

Wood choice

I had used lime (*Tilia vulgaris*) for all of my previous work, a wood traditionally used by carvers and modellers. I knew it could be worked precisely, it was easy to cut, turn, carve, and if necessary polished well to give a good surface.

As well as carving curvilinear forms to represent landscapes, it allowed me to make thin, delicate components and leaves. It presented no problems when modelling and did not split or distort on completion.

The consistent lightness of colour of the wood, and its uniform, close grain gave emphasis to the overall form and the most intricate detail. At the same time, its mellow and subtle surface made it very tactile to work.

Having a stock of good quality lime has been essential over the years and I have made a point of building up a range of planks of various thicknesses. W L West and Son Ltd, timber merchants and importers based in Selham, West Sussex always provide very good quality English lime for carvers and are helpful when supplying small quantities.

Carving process

I have a Startrite combination saw bench, planer thicknesser, morticer and spindle moulder which I have found a totally reliable and versatile machine, enabling me to process the timber very easily.

I work systematically. I saw the wood to the correct size, square it up and mark the dimensions using my original drawings and notes.

I rough out using a large 1in, 25mm gouge to remove enough wood to reveal the overall form of the piece. The next stage is to cut the wood more closely to the original markings and block in the details. I finally use smaller gouges to work the surface to the required finish.

Big picture **Artichoke is 4in, 10cm in circumference**
Opposite top **Together with the *Snail Shell* and *Drain*, this mainly turned temple forms a triptych. They were made from one piece of lime**
Opposite above **Snail Shell is 9 x 9in, 23 x 23cm**
Above **Drain is a carved landscape which has been left raw rather than sealed**

Dolphin Head Fountain at the Weald and Downland Museum

Although I have collected a range of chisels and gouges which are sometimes required for a particular job, I tend to work with half a dozen tools, three straight gouges ¼–⅜in, 6–10mm in size, two skew chisels and a V tool. I have become familiar with them and the more I use them the more versatile they become for most tasks, using only a fraction of the blade to work the detail.

I am frequently asked how long it takes to complete each piece. In the past, the carver, like any other tradesman, would have worked to a price. There is an assumption that anything hand-made takes a long time.

Because of the research time given to me by Kingston University and the support from various sponsors, I have never considered the work to be a commercial venture in any sense. Its function would, however, be educational, albeit in an enigmatic way.

Echoes exhibition

The choice of where to show the work was, I thought, a key factor in extending my research. The first venue was the Weald and Downland Open-air Museum at Singleton, West Sussex in spring 1995. The museum's aim is to save threatened buildings and exhibit them so visitors can appreciate the rich heritage of historic buildings in the region.

My exhibition was housed in the upper hall from Crawley, a magnificent timber-framed building which may have been a meeting place. This fitted in exactly with my idea of the fragments I had made being brought together.

My work was able to help generate an increased public awareness and interest in the relationship between the buildings and the natural environment.

The second venue provided a contrasting cultural background. The National Trust at Petworth House is surrounded by Capability Brown landscape and houses artworks of international importance, including a carved room containing the work of Grinling Gibbons.

Diana Owen, Property Manager for the house, suggested the work could be shown in the Education gallery during October. Like the Weald and Downland Museum, the audience showed concern about tradition, continuity and skills. They were interested to see a contemporary use of wood as a way of expressing ideas about current issues and familiar surroundings.

On both occasions, I met members of the public who wanted to have a go at making something and I advised them on the choice of timber, tools and subject matter. I talked to younger people about the possible ways of developing their talents through the education system and what kind of courses to pursue.

Both sites offered their own particular stimulus and I produced several interpretations of the artefacts I had observed on both sites. I recreated mechanical and man-made objects in miniature and presented small, natural forms such as snail shells and birds' skulls to a larger scale, giving them an architectural presence.

In *Pike with Boathouse* and *Artichoke with Temple* I used three-dimensional perspective to establish a new relationship between objects of varying scale within the same composition.

Artistic approach

As in any creative process, choice and editing play an important part in my working process. Sometimes I have a plan of action. More often than not I don't seek, I find. A balance of control and intuition, sketching, measured drawings, quick sketch maquettes and photographs form the basis of the final composition.

I always work on three or four pieces simultaneously, contrasting in scale and complexity, perhaps a large organic form alongside a minute complex structure.

Ideas flow from one to the other providing common ground as well as contrasting forms. This formula also provides a varied work programme and drives me to complete the work fairly quickly.

If possible, I like to work outside, near to my subject, and I have taken advantage of various situations in my garden. I found I could get a better description of waterlilies, ponds and reeds if I stood among them as I carved the wood to the right shape.

If artefacts were farther afield, I was more dependent on drawings but, at the end of the day in the workshop, I needed to return to check for measurements and proportions, and to re-establish a bond with the place or the object.

My priorities are closeness, both with the subject and with the working process, drawing, using my hands, simple tools, wood and understanding its limitations, pushing to the limits and testing myself. These join me closely with my past, present and the future. ●

Ted Vincent is a Senior Lecturer in the School of Three-dimensional Design at Kingston University in Surrey. He is happy to advise anyone entering an education in three-dimensional design.

Bob Ayers' showroom displays his rustic style of work

COACH AND CARVER

HUGH FOSTER

Bob Ayers works as a full-time teacher and coach, and runs a carving business as well; he's a man who works as a hobby.

Bob Ayers has found the secret of success. He works hard at it. Skill? He developed it by working at his craft. Talent? He says it's not a question of talent, but of pride: 'I'm putting my *name* on every piece I make.'

Even so, skill and talent aren't enough. Ayers knows that the secret is time, and he puts in lots of time. He's a full-time teacher and coach, so he can carve only 40-50 hours a week while school is on, rather than the 80 hours plus he works during school holidays. He leaves home early each morning, to put in an hour or two carving before going to school. On his way home from school, he goes to the studio again, and puts in another three or four hours. One might reasonably

Bob Ayers cleaning up a sign before painting

claim that Bob's business is his hobby, or vice versa. It's a good thing his wife doesn't view him as a workaholic! He reminds me of the old saw: 'Small business is where a fellow works 80 hours a week for himself to avoid working 40 hours a week for someone else.' How true, how true!

When I drove past his shop late one Christmas morning, he was there, working. Is this just dedication, fanaticism, or does the secret of success go beyond time to a simple fact? The main reason that Bob Ayers is good at what he does, is that he loves doing it. This love has to be the secret of every successful business-person, no matter what persuasion.

There are visitors in the carving studio at least half the time. Sometimes they're customers, but more of the time, they're friends, former students, people who come in to see what's playing on the TV (you can be sure it's a sporting event of some kind), to chat, or to watch Bob work. He says that when company is present, he's not really working, though he continues to carve. He chats, but seldom makes very good eye contact, unless he has a real point to make in the conversation. The tools are sharp and he must watch what he's doing. He carves without appearing to make a great effort. It's less that the carving is so easy, more that he's very well disciplined. Visitors may not realise how much Bob is doing, until they see the stacks of plaques that have accumulated during the visit.

Finished and ready for a customer's wall

Time and price

Time relates directly to one of his major observations about selling. Too many craftspeople equate selling price with the amount of time they have invested in the project. He says there's virtually no correlation. A product's price is determined by the market. He'd rather sell two items at $129 than not sell two at $229. If $129 is what the market will bear, the only people who will do well are those who can profitably make the product at that price.

One of his main carving talents is a willingness to re-do a project until it strikes him as being right. After all, as he says, his reputation relies on the quality of his work. One piece, reworked several times, still left him unsatisfied. One day a fellow from out of town stopped in, saw it on the floor, and asked how much. In sheer frustration, Ayers said: 'Take it. Get it out of here!' He wrote it off as advertising — it generated nearly a dozen-and-a-half other sales for similar items. The fellow who got it is one of the best walking adverts anyone could have.

One of Bob Ayers' most famous projects has been the Ducks Unlimited table. When he first conceived the project, they were sold only at a hunting club's annual auction. The prices were very high, perhaps high enough to move them from the realm of craft to the realm of art. The table is a massive 2ft x 5ft, made up of mitred four-by-fours, the overall height if the table is 19⅝in. Ayers has the tables built for him, as he claims he's not a woodworker. When last questioned, he paid

a furnituremaker $300 for the assembled table. To that he adds some glass, an old gun, some dried flowers, and some carvings. The table leaves his shop $1,000 (or more) heavier than it comes in.

Bob Ayers doesn't sharpen his own tools; claims he doesn't know how. He pays someone to do this, as he earns less when he's sharpening, far less than when he's carving. It's probably smart to specialise like this. Leave the jobs at which we're not expert to those who are. That leaves us free to develop our most profitable skills.

Bob Ayers has had no formal training,

The table is made by a furniture maker, Bob Ayers adds the carvings and other items under the glass top

Memories signs have appropriate items of sports wear as the focal point

Sign boards are popular with customers

the home of the Green Bay Packers American football team; located in the smallest city to host a professional team, the Packers have an avid following of supporters. When people started ordering carved 'Packer' memorabilia, Bob realised that he was on to a good thing; he put out a few extra pieces in his shop and now the sports wall-plaque business has taken-off.

One day a man came in looking for directions. While Bob was giving the directions, the person seeking them looked around in his shop. He then mentioned that he had a sports shop in suburban Chicago, and was confident that he could sell half a dozen or so wall plaques similar to the Packers model in the shop, if only they said Bears or Cubs. He was so confident that he put his money where his mouth was and, before he left, had written a sizable cheque for the order. This order was quickly filled, and almost as quickly sold out. There followed another, larger order. Then the orders started coming in from other sports shops, near other teams. Bob says that he has now carved logos for nearly every professional sports team, and for the more popular college and university teams.

Advertising? A couple of times a year Bob Ayers sends half-a-dozen sets of photos to large vendors, figuring that if one or two of them 'bite', he'll have more work. Even better, though, is word of mouth. People call him, saying, 'If you can make that wonderful Cubs logo, surely you can make me one that says . . .' He can and he will.

It was almost by accident that this year's two main products appeared. Over the years, he had learned that the secret of making the Ducks Unlimited table was getting people to scrounge up old rifles for him. Now he has people hunting for old baseball gloves and caps, and US Civil War (and re-enactment) hats. These are used to carve this year's 'legacy' series. He's gearing up for another 'legacy' series next year on different topics.

Bob Ayers believes people who run small businesses should expect to make lots of mistakes when they act on impulse, rather than relying on expertise in marketing, accounting, budgeting, and the like. In 20 years, Ayers has made his share of mistakes, but has profited by working hard. When he doesn't like the way a project turns out, he changes it. Sometimes he's asked about leaving teaching: 'The kids are too important,' he says, 'and not enough people pay real attention to them.' When he's teaching or coaching, the kids get the same percentage of his best effort as does his carving. Of course, teaching is very steady work, a vocation that appeals to that portion that requires stability. ∎

he picked up what he knows by experimentation, watching others work, and by paying attention. He says much of what he does comes from somewhere, perhaps a gift from a higher power; most of us only wish to be so gifted. While we're wishing, he's busy doing, and he does a lot, for he carves upwards of a thousand projects per year. When carving fish, he says, that six completed projects per day is decent output.

Years ago, he says, he needed a shop near a museum. Today, his shop is in an out-of-the-way, mostly residential neighbourhood. Sometimes people come in by accident, because they are looking for something else, because they are lost, or sometimes even because they are looking for him. He gets lots of orders, and lots of people who know someone who just needs one of his wares.

Sports sales

Since he lives in northeastern Wisconsin, where deer and ducks, hunting and fishing are popular pastimes, a wildlife motif appears in much of his work, though the coach and sports-fan comes out in Bob Ayers' carving. Northeastern Wisconsin is

Below **Man At Bus Stop,** carved in plane
Right **A garden fountain carved in plane**
Opposite below **A small walled town
carved from a piece of pear tree**

Suzy Placet discovers
the vibrant and humorous
imagination of Pierre Décorse

THE ENC

T he drive through the huge variety of woods to
Pierre Décorse's house should have given me a
clue as to what to expect in the variety of his
work, but nothing prepared me for the surprise
that was waiting.

I entered the garden where his workshop and house lay
nestled in the lush French countryside, and the first thing I
saw was a larger-than-life sized figure in a long overcoat and
cap with a carpet bag, leaning against a crooked lamp post.
He looked as if he was waiting for a bus!

On closer inspection I discovered this imposing figure
was carved out of a plane tree (*Platanus hybrida*). The wood
shone richly in the sun and looked as if it had just been
carefully polished. Other characters and animals occupied the
garden, but the father of them all was nowhere to be seen.

Eventually I found Pierre asleep in his hammock in the
spring sunshine, pipe in hand, and no doubt dreaming up
even more outlandish and delightful creations. He
welcomed me warmly, his eyes sparkling with fun. It was
difficult to ask pertinent questions because I was so
mesmerized by what I saw and, it seems, I am not alone.

For the past eight years Pierre Décorse has been
carving and sculpting everything he can lay his hands
on. He has frequent exhibitions in the region and sells
practically everything he produces, as visitors cannot
resist the aesthetic pleasure his sculptures give.

Joyful creation

Pierre's main ingredient to such a successful, newly acquired
occupation is joy. Fundamentally this former accountant is a

ANTED WOOD

happy person and it shows blatantly in his work. Unlike many other carvers he doesn't try to 'tame' his wood to fit his requirements, but bends his concept to conform with the wood's natural formation. He is totally self-taught and this explains his spontaneity and unconventional attitude towards carving.

As we wandered from one carving to the next I became more and more enchanted. I asked him what kind of wood he used.

"Everything", he answered. "How about this?" I said, pointing to a strange-looking fountain sitting in the middle of the workshop. Four branches stemmed upwards from a bowl into which a trickle of water ran. Inside the bowl a minute mermaid reclined on the water's edge and on

the top a small man sat, crouched, arms around his knees, looking down at the girl.

It turned out the base was made of elm (*Ulmus spp*) and the bowl was of olive (*Olea europaea*), dried over 20 years. The branches were a mixture of beech (*Fagus sylvatica*) and juniper, and the figures were of yet another wood. He finds his wood locally and although he uses elm, plane, beech and chestnut (*Aesculus hippocastanum*) extensively he admits to a preference for working with fruit tree woods.

His work is as varied as his choice of wood. A small, walled town with crooked roofs and chimneys erupted from what looked like a pumpkin but was really an interesting piece of pear tree (*Pyrus communis*) which had captured his imagination. A kernel, opened to expose a castle, was carved from a heather root.

I came across strange ships and inventions, a stranded train in the desert overtaken by a man and his camel, insects and animals. All were carved out of woods from the surrounding countryside and the extraordinary, fertile imagination of this unique artist.

Experimental evolution

I wanted to get to the root of his knowledge. Who had taught him? Where did he study? But there was nothing to learn as he told me he had just experimented over the years. He went from large sculptures, cut to preliminary shape with a chainsaw and carved with classical tools, to working his way into the Lilliputian world of miniature pieces using dentist's equipment.

Pierre makes tools to fit the piece he is working on and his powers of improvisation seem to know no bounds. He manages to bring out the richness of the colours of the wood by applying a coat of transparent anti-rust. The satin, polished patina he achieves comes, quite simply, from a coat of matt varnish on top of this.

A few years ago he made a couple of book ends from hazel and pear. A book shop owner happened to see them and bought them for his window display. Since then he has been asked to produce several similar pieces on a regular basis. They have proved so much in demand he has become obsessed by books and has produced hundreds of amusing sculptures on the subject. Among other works that sell well are beautiful chess sets, carved with such detail it takes your mind off the game.

Photo by Patricia Décorse

Left **Book ends in fruit wood**
Below **A giant-sized butterfly carved in plane**
Right *Page Turning*

Mandarin

A couple of years ago he went to China and was fascinated with what he found. You can see how their ivory carvings have influenced his work. On his return he carved a life-sized mandarin out of walnut which now stands sentinel outside his workshop, reminding him of his exotic travels.

Some of his inspiration is derived from nature. A huge butterfly can be seen in the high grass around the back of the house, and mushrooms, smooth and rust-coloured, sprout up here and there.

His obvious pleasure in discovering a new piece of wood is infectious. I wanted to start right there and then. Did he give courses? "No, I could never do that. I wouldn't know how to teach carving".

But his sense of humour is reflected in everything he does. For example I asked him about his man at the bus stop. He explained that following week he would be putting it down on the side of the main road. For many years the villagers had been asking for a local bus service but to no avail. "Now, at least", he said, with a twinkle in his eye, "there's someone waiting for a bus so maybe one will come along one day". If it ever does I expect it will be a wooden one! ●

Pierre Décorse was born in 1953 in the southern French town of Perpignan near the Spanish border on the Mediterranean coast. After his education he became a chartered accountant and continued his career until 1986. From simple whittling at the age of 17, which led to carving pendants, he nurtured a desire for woodcarving which finally got the better of him at the age of 35. He abandoned the office and set up a workshop in a tiny hamlet in the Lot area (east of the Dordogne) where he now lives with his wife and two children and carves full-time.

Roger Schroeder talks to
Carl Johnson who has
enjoyed carving humorous
figures for 50 years

Even after 50 years of carving, Carl Johnson of Queens, New York, USA, still has no trouble finding new and often humorous ideas for his pieces. His work ranges from portraits of people (some in funny situations) to nearly life-size figures and diminutive folk characters.

Johnson's interest in art goes back to his teens when he took up a pencil and drew cartoons. During those years he also tried his hand at carving model aeroplanes. He recalls using wooden matches for the struts of the models.

The Painter, inspired by an accident Johnson had on a ladder

This piece was inspired by the King Arthur legend and the Minnesota Vikings football team

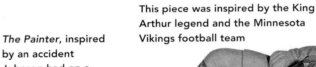

HUMOROUS H

Left **Johnson's carving of woodsculptor Armand LaMontagne at work on Larry Bird**

In his early 20s, he started working for the aircraft and defence industry. There he was able to carve for a living by making models for wind tunnel tests. It was precision work, he says, and included making scale models of aeroplanes, missiles and even space capsules.

Today, aged 78, he still builds models, most recently boats, and adeptly handles a knife or gouge. He does carvings for family, friends and customers and is much in demand.

Painter's plight

What kinds of carvings does Johnson favour?

"I like to make humorous figures, ones which are not too stiff," he says. He refers frequently to a caricature of a painter, a figure he has done in life-size and miniature. The painter and his paint bucket were both entangled in his ladder.

This sorry plight was inspired by a near fatal incident that happened to Johnson. He relates how he was two storeys up on a ladder, chasing squirrels from his attic. A combination of mishaps led to 11 broken bones on one side of his body.

The ladder was propped against the corner of the house, and a squirrel, which was not happy about being poked with a broom handle, jumped at his face. Even while he was incapacitated, with one hand in a cast, Johnson was working on *The Painter*. Some years later, he was commissioned to carve a larger version for a paint store.

Local heroes

Another humorous piece was inspired by the unlikely combination of the Minnesota Vikings football team and the legend of King Arthur. One of King Arthur's exploits was removing the sword Excalibur from a great stone. The story says only the rightful king would be able to withdraw it.

Johnson replaced Arthur with a Norse Viking who pulled so hard on the sword he tipped the rock and himself over. The reason for the switch? It was a gift for Johnson's son, a Viking football fan.

Another carving was of an organ grinder and a monkey sitting on a park bench. Each figure held a sore foot. Johnson remembers seeing street entertainers as a child, so it was not a hard composition to conjure up. Carved in 1982, he called the piece *Mutual Sympathy*.

He also carves portraits of people, especially those who work wood. I enjoy furniture making, so Johnson carved me at my cabinetmaker's bench. Although the miniature bench was built rather than carved, it was an exact replica of one in maple (*Acer spp*) with actual vices which screwed and unscrewed.

After he met American woodsculptor Armand LaMontagne, Johnson carved the artist in miniature, sculpting basketball superstar Larry Bird.

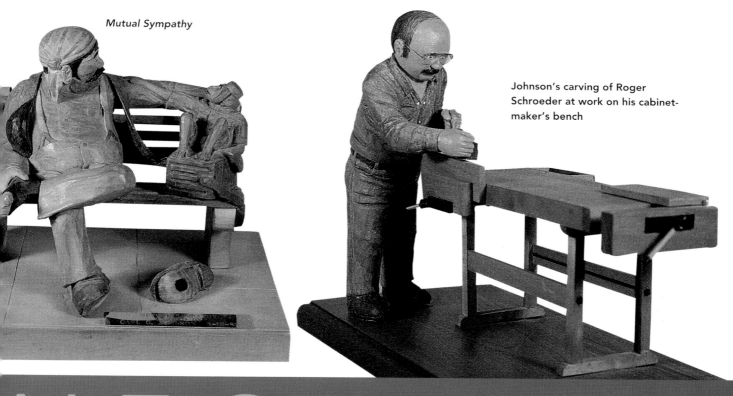

Mutual Sympathy

Johnson's carving of Roger Schroeder at work on his cabinet-maker's bench

Above **Johnson begins painting the bagpiper by painting the flesh tones, using a mix of a Windsor and Newton acrylic called medium portrait pink and Liquitex's unbleached titanium** Below **For the boy's shirt, Johnson applies unbleached titanium and for the shorts Liquitex's phthalocyanine blue**

Above **Carl Johnson paints the bagpiper and curious boy** Below ***Nosy Kid** or **Does He Or Doesn't He?***

Pipe dream

One of Johnson's most popular pieces is a Scottish bagpiper and a little boy peering under the kilt. It may have been inspired by photos of bagpipers, but wherever the idea came from, Johnson was looking to do an animated carving that would get a laugh. He had two possible titles for this piece, *Nosy Kid* or *Does He Or Doesn't He?*.

Johnson paints his pieces using acrylics. Mixed with water, they produce washes which can be applied and re-applied for different intensities of colour, and they dry in minutes. Johnson demonstrated on the bagpiper, showing how he could paint the entire piece in just two hours. ●

Roger Schroeder is a prolific writer and lecturer on woodworking, construction, sculpture and carving, as well as a cabinet-maker and amateur carver. He combines these activities with a full-time job as a high school English teacher, specialising in teaching creative writing and research.

Alicia Beesley learns how a wide range of tools and techniques are used to create Jim Hare's dramatic sculptures

Left **Eagle and prey**
Below left
**The Wild Horse,
Jim's first carving**

POWER CUTS

Browsing round a local art centre recently I found an amazing sculpture by Jim Hare. It was a carving called *Amore*, a column of symbolic content in the celebration of love. I was rather surprised as I had thought of Jim only as a painter, so I arranged to visit his studio to photograph some of his other woodcarvings.

I was rather taken aback at the number of carvings Jim had to show me. I asked him if he had a favourite piece. "Not as such, as they all have a special meaning for me, but this one called *Embrace* I particularly like", he said. "See how the loving, tender features intertwine, incorporating all the close feelings of emotion.

"I enjoy this type of work. It takes you away from finicky, tiny imagery which can be tiresome. This is where the excitement of power tools comes in."

Poetic piece

Next was a commissioned piece made for a local fiddle group called the Gallowvidians, celebrating the life and works of the poet Robert Burns. It was to be a gift to the Annapolis Burns Federation in America.

Jim made it using a bandsaw and chisels, and it incorporated five different types of wood: sycamore (*Acer pseudoplatanus*) for the book, ash (*Fraxinus spp*) for the pen, beech (*Fagus spp*) for the inkwell, yew (*Taxus baccata*) for the fiddle, and elm (*Ulmus spp*) for the base.

When he cut into the leaves of the book they started to curl on their own. Being so thin, there must have been tension in the wood, and fortunately in this case it made the piece much more realistic.

It became apparent that to do full justice to the enthusiasm and vitality of this quiet 70-year-old I would have to return, so a few days later I met Jim again in his workshop. It reminded me of Dr Who's Tardis. A small door on the outside wall opened into a spacious room. Lots of equipment lay around and a fair depth of sawdust and wood shavings littered the floor.

I asked him about his wood. "Most of the hardwood timber I get from local sawmills. On occasions I've managed to find some beautiful pieces from near the root systems and of no commercial value. These pieces can produce the most remarkable abstract forms with exquisite grain", he told me.

"When I envisage a particular sculpture

Above **Embrace**

Right **Amore, a sculptured column symbolising the celebration of love**

I select the timber with the greatest care. Experience has taught me that moisture content, internal stresses and such things as nails or fencing wire embedded in the wood can have disastrous results when carved."

Special seal

Jim follows a strict routine when preparing his timber. After it has been cut to the required dimensions it is end sealed and stored in an airy room to dry. His end sealing is unconventional, but he says it works.

After cutting, the wood is laid aside for a week or two for the surface face to dry. He then applies hot paraffin wax, but he only applies the end sealant to 2 or 3in, 50 to 75mm from the outer edge of the wood, leaving the centre of the end face clear. He then applies the wax on all four sides for about 6 to 8in, 150 to 180mm from each end.

As the centre core of the wood is the last to dry out, Jim has found the outside edges dry out and shrink quickly. Not being able to shrink around the moist core it cracks, and when a crack starts, it runs.

With his method, moisture is trapped by the sealant wax where cracking would normally start, but it allows the core to dry out, thus minimising the chance of splitting. Since air drying takes about a year per 1in, 25mm diameter, the date when first stored is marked on each piece.

The *Shakespeare Column* depicting characters from his works

Timber choice

When I asked Jim about his favourite timber he said: "I don't have any preferences really. Every wood has features, be it texture, colour or grain, which never fail to intrigue me and stimulate my curiosity.

"I feel if we get too rigid about our likes and dislikes of particular woods we lose the excitement of one more facet of the art element in our craft. I choose wood to suit the piece, but I still retain my curiosity about others. I suppose I always will."

Continuing process

I realised Jim's intensity and enthusiasm came from more than just a craft involvement. Here was someone who loved the art in woodcarving. His aesthetic appreciation of the finished form was so intense, there had to be something more than just the visual response.

"I take every element of my creative ability in woodcarving to a personal level. As I sculpt I am aware the timber has been a living, breathing, growing tree, and the form I create from it is a continuation of that process.

"Not long ago I carved a falcon from an oak beam (*Quercus spp*) recovered during renovation of a castle keep built in 1425. The old oak was probably growing 100 years before that, so my falcon was a continuation, 700 years on and still going strong.

Next Jim showed me his current project, a 5ft, 1.5m column of elm 12in, 305mm square. To approach this was daunting to say the least, never mind create a sculpture from it. It was to be a portrait of many of the characters conjured up in that great Robert Burns classical narrative *Tam O Shanter*.

He planned to begin at the top with Burns' portrait, and bring in all the exciting characters portrayed in the poem as he worked down the column.

Power tools

Jim selected a power tool from the bench. "I always start a big one with this", he confided. "This" was an Arbortech disc which cut the wood away almost as fast as a chainsaw. I watched from behind a clear polythene sheet as Jim adjusted his protective goggles and mask and cut the first groove in the block.

He cut deep grooves down to about 8in, 200mm from the top of the column, leaving about ⅛in, 3mm between each groove. Then he feathered the blade from side to side, taking away the ridges left by the first cuts. The result was a clear removal of wood 1in, 25mm deep from the top to 8in, 200mm down one side. "The little ridges I leave keep the blade from slipping back into the previous cut", he explained.

I was aware of a great change in Jim as he picked up the Arbortech. Gone was his lively outgoing attitude. His every move had become clinical as he handled this effective machine. No cut was made at random.

I commented on this and for a moment he seemed apologetic. "It's probably an instinctive survival response", he explained. "Craftsmen come to have a great respect for their power tools and work with care. One mistake can be too many. When I pick up a power tool I hurry slowly", he laughed.

The involvement and enthusiasm Jim had for his woodcarving rubbed off on me. A few days later I returned to his workshop to get a better understanding of how he used the tools he had shown me.

Top **Jim's method of end sealing timber leaves the centre of the end face clear of sealing wax**
Centre **Cutting ridges with the Arbortech**
Bottom **After cutting deep grooves, Jim feathers the Arbortech blade from side to side taking away the ridges left by the first cuts**

Cheating time

He had an Arbortech, hand drill, mini drill, jigsaw, flexible shaft tool, and small attachments such as burrs, bits, augers, flap wheel sanders plus innumerable small cutters and other devices specially designed for specific purposes.

I was impressed by this array of gadgets and asked what chisels he used. "I hardly ever use chisels or gouges now. At my age I am working against the clock", he said. "Gouges are a bit slow and tedious to me now. They are wonderful tools really, but I have so many ideas, a sense of urgency almost takes over.

"One facet of creative three dimensional art I have found, is inspiration comes in spasmodic bursts. I think this is true with most artists, and the drive and excitement which accompanies it almost assures us of a fine artwork.

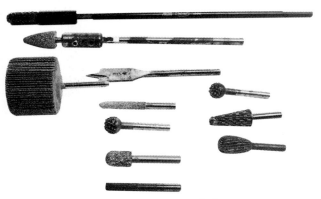

Some of the attachments Jim uses regularly

"At other times your creativity can be on a flat, and at those times it is better to walk away. While the sense of urgency persists and the image is clear in the mind, then the power tools get you there, or at least to the finishing stage.

"In painting, the excellence or otherwise of the finished canvas lies in the craft ability of handling the paint and brushes with skill. The same applies to carving tools."

Flexible friend

Jim showed me a handy, versatile tool, a flexible drive shaft made by Wolfcraft. He explained the central core of the shaft transmitted the power from a motor to the chuck at the other end and allowed the carver to bring the cutter to the work from any direction.

Many implements could be fitted into the chuck for either cutting, sanding or fine drilling. One home-made implement he used regularly was made from a 6in, 150mm nail with the head cut off. The nail was wrapped in masking tape, then a piece of sanding belt was cut to length and fixed with superglue round the nail. An inch of nail was left for gripping in the chuck.

Only one layer of sanding belt was needed, with the glued down edge on the trailing side of the rotation. The masking tape was needed to ensure a good grip to the nail. This tool could reach into the most inaccessible places, and a vast range of sizes and grades could be made cheaply.

A home made sanding tool made from a nail, masking tape and some sanding belt

Jim said a good range of cutting tools and accessories was available commercially from tool shops or by looking at the advertisements in **Woodcarving**. He mentioned a nice range of tungsten burrs by Rod Naylor, and an extension bar from Marples which would take most implements.

"The bar is 12in, 305mm long x ¼in, 6mm diameter. At one end there is a 2in, 50mm steel tube with grub screws to hold the cutter. I used this bar extensively for deep cutting and sanding the *Shakespeare Column* behind the figures. It can be fitted to a hand drill or a flexible drive shaft", he said.

The jigsaw blade covered with masking tape and some sanding belt

Watching Jim demonstrate all these carving tools with speed and dexterity, I could well understand his excitement and enthusiasm for carving. He also showed me a jigsaw blade covered with a piece of sanding belt. The teeth of the old blade had been ground off, and it was covered with masking tape before the abrasive was glued on. There was an extra ¼in, 6mm protruding over the tip of the blade to keep it from digging into the wood. "This is a very fast flat sander and it can reach into very narrow spaces", he said.

Power tool problems

I asked Jim if he had any problems with power tools. The only big problem he had was with the flexible drive shaft when he was working with a burr which stuck in a tight corner. The motor continued to turn the central core of the flexible drive shaft and the core either broke or the whole shaft twisted so tight it became unusable.

To minimise this problem he slackened the belt drive from the motor until it just drove and no more, without slipping. If the tool stuck, the belt slipped like a slipping clutch and prevented damage to the drive shaft.

Beating cracks

The main problem with wood was splitting. This could be frustrating if it happened when a piece was almost finished. Many types of wood, although perfectly dry, would distort or twist when stresses were released by carving. Small cracks were common and these could be filled or glued, but larger cracks needed more drastic treatment.

"To minimise the damage I drill a hole in the wood at right angles to the crack, and in past the crack for an inch or two. I insert a length of dowel or studding ¼in, 6mm shorter than the depth of the hole and a good fit. This is heavily coated with Araldite or similar adhesive and pushed right in

as far as it will go. The hole is then plugged with a similar piece of wood and the whole thing is then clamped firmly in a bench vice for a day or two until the adhesive has cured.

"This stops the split from opening, and sometimes it can be almost invisible. In the carving world, cracks in the wood are seen as an acceptable feature, although in fine sculptures they attract the eye and distract from the aesthetic impact of the piece."

Artistic fulfilment

Having watched enthralled as Jim worked, explained and enthused with such intensity, almost demanding at times, I was beginning to understand every line, silhouette, movement, surface finish and intrinsic emotion in his carvings. I got the feeling there was much more to it than just achieving the finished carving.

"There is no beginning or end in creative art", he said. "From the first idea and line drawing of the sculpture to the finished piece there are so many facets of emotion, tension, mood, frustration and weary concentration before we reach the final service finish and stand back with a sigh to admire our masterpiece.

"But no one ever knows if they have created their best sculpture. What we do know is in each piece is the fulfilment of all the emotions, creativity, craftsmanship and effort we can muster, and probably a fortnight of our life well spent."

By this time Jim's infectious enthusiasm for his craft and his desire to share all the tricks of the trade had left a lasting impression. As I left his workshop I realised I had become hooked on carving. ●

Jim Hare was born in 1925 near Lanark and studied tool design in relation to industrial plastics, but had a love of art from boyhood. He retired from desk work in 1980 and moved to Clarencefield where he set up a studio/workshop to concentrate on painting, and then wood sculpture. He is a member of the Dumfries and Galloway Fine Arts Society and the British Woodcarvers Association. One of Scotland's best known carvers, his work can be found in collections around the world.

Arbortech supplied by BriMarc Associates, 8 Ladbroke Park, Millers Road, Warwick CV34 5AE. Tel: 01926 493389
Wolfcraft Ltd are at The Granary, Walnut Tree Lane, Sudbury, Suffolk CO10 6BD. Tel: 01787 880776
Tungsten burrs from Rod Naylor, 208 Devizes Road, Hilperton, Trowbridge, Wiltshire BA14 7QP. Tel: 01225 754497

WHERE THERE'S A WILL

With no workshop, few tools and little money, but plenty of enthusiasm, Adam Styles is establishing his own identity as a carver

Remembering my first experience of carving and my enthusiasm before I even started the piece, it was as if I knew then how I would grow to love carving and the part it would play in my life. It was the autumn of 1987. I already had a ¾in curved gouge and a square carpenters mallet and now, thanks to a slightly apprehensive friend who helped me roll a large log from one end of the school grounds to the other, I had the wood. I was all set to start carving the next day. That night I was too excited to sleep.

But in the morning I found there had been such a bad storm that the school was closed. After three days of frustration it eventually reopened and I got stuck into the carving. I think it took me three or four weeks to complete. The whole carving was done with just that one gouge.

Since then I have been prolific, working in all sizes, on all manner of subjects and in different woods. Every piece is still approached with the same raw enthusiasm as the very first.

Second-hand tools

Naturally when producing a wide range of work it becomes necessary to have the right tools. My collection has grown slowly over six years. I buy as and when I need something and if my wallet permits, and now have around twenty five chisels and gouges.

Luckily I have realised that carving doesn't have to be expensive, quite the opposite in fact. You can find excellent second-hand tools at very good prices in markets, boot-sales and sometimes old workshops that are closing down. They may look old and rusty but when cleaned up they are likely to be of superior steel, have better handles and be generally much more hard-wearing than many of the new tools on the market today. I do buy new chisels as well, mainly when something specific is required. I think my largest outlay on tools was £40 for a set of Henry Taylor gouges.

Personal touch

My workshop consists of a dustsheet and a Black and Decker Workmate in the corner of my bedroom, or if the weather is fine or it is a large piece I work in the back garden. I much prefer to be in the fresh air rather than in the more conventional workshop atmosphere.

For carving purposes and flexibility, I have found that my legs are the best workbench and clamps available. It gives me a more personal relationship with the work, and I don't like constantly having to fiddle around opening and closing a vice and adjusting the carving and padding, only to have to do it again a few minutes later. Obviously there are certain situations in which a vice or clamp cannot be avoided, but whenever possible I use my legs to hold the work.

Recycled materials

When starting out, I was not at all fussy about what wood I carved – after all, a piece of wood was a piece of wood. But as I have become more experienced I find that I have subconsciously become more selective, to the point where I am only interested in certain types of timber, mainly hardwoods. This is another issue regarding money, and for me it

surfaced while I was preparing to carve *The Head*. I wanted to do it considerably larger than a human head and from a dry, seasoned oak to minimise cracking. I simply couldn't afford to buy a piece of oak, so I had to think of something else.

I found some second-hand four by five oak fence posts. After sawing these up and discarding the rotten areas, I was left with eight lengths of 18in, 450mm. I took them indoors where they stood for a month to lose most of their moisture content. They were then planed square and left for a further two weeks. After a second planing, they were ready for joining. Using Cascamite adhesive I glued three lengths together, then another three and finally the other two. So now I had three pieces. These were planed and glued to form the block.

Mini-Van. **The hardest project, an accurate copy, down to the details of antenna and trimmings in oak veneer. Most of it was carved by eye, only taking measurements when absolutely necessary**

Waste not

Surprisingly there was very little movement from the block throughout the carving process. After the success of this experiment, I have used this method of building a carvable block from a number of smaller ones on numerous occasions. The *Egg Man* and the *Mini-Van*, both also made from oak, started life as gate posts.

As well as using wood from fencing and gates I have also found hardwoods suitable for carving on skips, building sites and even just lying in the street. Another good source is old furniture, table legs and so on. Admittedly I have

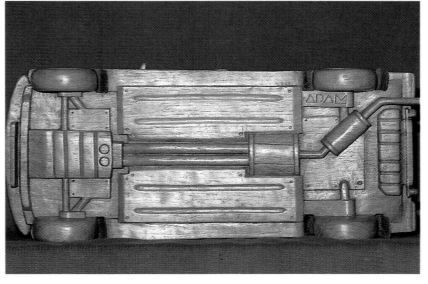

Adam Styles has been carving wood for just over six years. While still at school he became tired of the flatness of painting and drawing and, inspired by one of his teachers, took up woodcarving. An increasing passion for three-dimensional work led to a Fine Art/Sculpture degree at Farnham School of Art, from where he graduated last July. Since then he has continued carving, sometimes to commission, while searching for the opportunity to use his skills in paid employment.

Right
The Head. Inspired by heavyweight boxer Mike Tyson, this became an abstract self-portrait. The block was made up of recycled oak fence posts, planed and glued together

only used this technique with oak and mahogany, but I see no reason why it should not work equally well for other timbers. Although not appropriate for all carvings, it is inexpensive and 'ecologically sound' at a time when the world's trees are being felled at a sickening rate.

Mini-Van

A friend of mine, who is a Mini enthusiast, asked if I would carve a replica of his van. I agreed, thinking that it would be an interesting challenge, although I had never carved an accurate representation before. I had no idea what I was letting myself in for.

It turned out to be the most difficult carving I had ever undertaken. I was working from photographs and it was very difficult to get a sense of scale. In the beginning, I measured everything before taking any wood away. I soon abandoned this approach because the photographs were all different sizes, it was too slow and I wasn't getting anywhere. So I took my life in my hands and carved everything by eye, only measuring when it was really important. This was quicker, more enjoyable and arguably more accurate.

Owing to the complexity of the subject, many parts had to be carved and sanded separately and glued on after the main carving was complete, particularly things like wing mirrors, fog lamps, doorhandles and so on. The whole carving is made from pieces from an oak gate post, except the mudflaps, trimming and antenna which are oak veneer. The finish is beeswax.

The Egg Man

When people first saw the Egg Man, many commented on a resemblance to the Greek mythological figure Atlas. In fact the original inspiration stemmed from another aspect of Greek culture, Cycladic art.

I enjoy working on semi-abstract human forms, so it seemed a good idea to try to create my own style of figure. I wanted the form to be simple and striking but at the same time with some uncertainty about it. There are three areas of uncertainty: the first is the sex of the figure; second is the egg, and whether it is in fact the head or is the figure simply holding it there; and the third – well, try to position your arms in the same way as the figure.

Originally I was uncertain whether I would actually carve the image, but as I wanted to take a mould and cast other editions in bronze and aluminium it seemed a good idea.

The wood is oak and comes from an old gate post, joined with Cascamite to obtain the correct size. The finish is two or three coats of

Egg Man. A simple, striking form, but with elements of ambiguity: is it male or female; is it a head or an egg; is the posture right?

beeswax polish. This particular figure stands 10in, 250mm high, but I have since carved a considerably larger version of the same design from an oak trunk, which stands approximately 60in, 1500mm high.

The Head

Images of the former heavyweight boxer, Mike Tyson, inspired me to begin this carving. I wanted to capture the power, aggression and the aura of the 'ring destroyer' that Tyson conveyed during his prime.

Ultimately it became a kind of abstract self-portrait, a very personal piece of work, while still preserving the aspects I originally wanted to capture in the carving. This is my favourite from all my carvings so far.

The block is constructed from eight lengths of fence post, joined with Cascamite. It stands 18in, 450mm high and again is finished with beeswax. ■

Ann and Bob Phillips were astonished by the scale and variety of subjects in Graham Pizzey's carvings

ALL CREATURES GREAT AND SMALL

Graham Pizzey is a carver trained in the traditional mould. His relief carvings of historical subjects are a feature of public buildings in his native New Zealand. His smaller scale relief work and sculptural works reach wider audiences, with examples in many countries around the world.

Graham's background made wood a natural medium to work with. His father was a furniture manufacturer, and although the young Graham wanted to go to art school his father advised him to learn a trade. As a compromise, he was apprenticed to his father by day as a cabinet maker, and by night he attended art classes.

Looking back, Graham says his daytime cabinet making taught him to deal with practicalities and gave him the attitude that has enabled him to keep afloat.

"Anything that came up in the way of hurdles became a challenge to be met. It was this outlook that kept me going when I was out on my own in later years. I didn't ever think when offered a contract 'I don't think I can manage this'. I just started, and got on with it. This survival instinct backed up the art school training. In short, Dad had it right." says Graham.

Hard times

"Just keep chipping away at it" could be his motto. A lifetime as a professional carver has meant lean times when it has been a struggle to raise his family. In his 25 years as a carver he has enjoyed both episodes of good fortune and many tough times.

He recalls suffering blistered feet from carrying samples of his work from gallery to gallery, times when contractors of huge commissions defaulted on payment leaving months of effort unrewarded, and episodes when only perseverance and a measure of cheek have topped up the family coffers!

On one occasion, after a tiring day trudging fruitlessly from shop to shop, he found his final prospect engaged in unwrapping a consignment of imported carvings. Graham threw out a last-resort challenge: "I'll take a bet. If you look at my work and don't order then I'll buy from you".

They say a salesman can never resist a good pitch. This time it paid off. Graham left with a full order book and didn't have to forfeit his slender funds to cover his bold wager.

Good training

Graham carves three-dimensional murals and sculptures covering an amazingly wide spectrum of subjects. His ability to handle a range of different media stems from his time served in an art studio after his apprenticeship.

The studio designers worked together on commercial design projects which were not only on a huge scale, but also involved using a wide variety of materials in combination with wood.

There are times when old buildings are a favoured subject, and a degree of athleticism is called for, plus a good head for heights. Over the years Graham has clambered in and out of rafters to gain a better perspective for large mural works.

Top **Graham Pizzey holding** *Pesky Heron,* **the bird he cut down to size, in white teak coloured with acrylic**
Above **Historic themed mural representing aspects of early life in a coastal town**

Material choice

For relief carvings Graham uses wood without a strong grain pattern to detract from the subject. The relatively bland grain of the teak family (*Tectona spp.*) fits the bill.

Graham's preferred material is white teak. For large carvings he laminates together planks measuring 12 x 2in, 300 x 50mm. He makes use of the grain for strength and also makes full use of the depth. In his relief carving detail for example, some areas are left with only a few millimetres depth remaining.

Tool junkies would have a field day in Graham's workshop. He uses only hand tools, and for a single carving he uses as many as 30 different chisels for the different cuts. Many he makes himself from old files, or Bendix springs out of a scrapped Bedford truck. A chisel made for one particular job might never be used again.

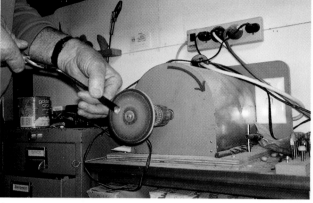

Below **The village *Smithy***
Top right **A selection of Graham's home-built tools**
Right **Graham sharpens the tool on a disc in the first stage of sharpening**

Sharpening is quickly achieved on a glass-polishing sanding disc. Graham is not one for laborious honing but we can vouch for the edge on his chisels.

Above **Working on a perspective model, Graham uses a minimum of sketched guides**

Sense of scale

The sheer size of his larger projects is daunting. Graham finds a "strong approach" is the best, if not the only way. His studies in perspective and anatomy at art school have been developed by practical experience.

He can turn a subject over in his head, look at it from different angles and see it from the back, all without sketching or modelling. Even on a large-scale mural Graham uses little more than a few perspective lines drawn in.

The murals illustrated here give an idea of the scale of work involved. The larger murals for example could be as much as 40ft, 12.2m long. Typical clients include public and private clubs and hotels. Often the subjects are historical and Graham has a fondness for old buildings as subjects.

His clients now include historical societies and he has made a piece for a private client of a historic farm homestead. The time spent on large projects is mind boggling. Some life-sized pieces have taken as much as nine months work to complete. The *Minstrel* measures 12 x 5ft, 3.6 x 1.5m.

Animal challenge

Kea, the Mountain Parrot shows the life-like detail

Outside historic subjects Graham enjoys wildlife carving, especially birds. Every bird presents a new challenge. He spent a week on the legs and claws of the *Kahu* (hawk) alone, finding much of the expressive tension of the sculpture was captured in the position of the feet and claws.

His work does not stop at the carved piece. Graham uses numerous coats of permanent oil stains to finish his bird sculptures. He has perfected the iridescent sheen of feathers by using a pearlising powder mixed with various tints as shown in *Kea* (mountain parrot).

This sculpture used 50 different mixing tints to satisfy Graham's demand for accuracy and he clocked up 500 hours on this particular piece.

Uninvited model

Graham didn't have to go far to find a model for his white heron sculpture. The heron arrived one morning, and over a period of days proceeded to raid his ornamental fish pond.

"I was torn between awe of its beauty and annoyance at its thievery. Finally I found it, uninvited, in my studio. That was the limit. I thought, I'll knock you down to size. I'll carve you". While the heron gorged on his goldfish Graham had ample opportunity to study every detail.

He tried especially to create the feeling of weightlessness. Each wing feather was individually carved to achieve this. "The bird was in my mind, perched. I didn't start to carve until I could see it clearly, front, back and even upside down".

Graham has had the last word. He knocked his adversary down to size by deliberately carving the heron at half size!

Carving has, on balance, not been the easiest of ways to make a living, but after all these years Graham has surprisingly few regrets. ●

For Glyn Mould, every new job – from complex restoration work to a simple house sign – brings a fresh challenge. Here he talks to Peter Pascoe

MEETING THE CHALLENGE

From the time he first held a carving chisel at the age of thirteen, Glyn Mould had no doubt what he wanted to do for a living. Seventeen years later, with a little help from a Government Enterprise Grant, and a lot of hard work, he is a respected professional woodcarver. He shares a converted stone-built Wesleyan Chapel dating from 1840 in the picturesque Northamptonshire village of Woodnewton.

Glyn is following a family tradition as his father is a stone carver. When he was a lad, Glyn would accompany his father all over the country helping out and watching as he worked on restoring stonework in churches.

Eventually his father bought him a set of woodcarving chisels and converted the garden shed into a workshop. Glyn never looked back. He admits that he is entirely self-taught – from reading every book on the subject he could buy or borrow, translating what he had seen his father do into woodcarving techniques, and experimenting – but mainly by observing.

A direct approach

When asked whether he felt he had lost out by not serving an apprenticeship or having 'proper' tuition, he said: 'I have not been trained to make a maquette in clay to develop my designs, and then copy it into wood as some schools teach. Therefore I have to do all my preparation and make my design decisions in my head, often designing on paper and then translating the ideas directly into wood. This makes for a more spontaneous and, I think, a more direct approach to the work. As my work is "jobbing" carving, where every job is different, and every job is a challenge, I think it works well.'

Glyn does tackle a wide range of projects. At the time of writing he was working on the restoration of a bishop's chair, a picture frame inspired by a period plaster frame, a plaque for the East Northamptonshire District Council, yet another village sign, this time in MDF, and preparing work for his stand at the East of England show. He also runs private classes, seminars and workshops in his studio.

Top right **Bishop's chair from Apethorpe church, before restoration**
Bottom right **Taking a scribed profile on acrylic sheet for the capital on the bishop's chair**
Far right **The completed capital, a faithful reproduction in terms of design, colour and patina**

Restoration complexity

According to Glyn, 'Restoration in itself is a vast subject, having many aspects. For instance, with the piece I am working on now, replacing a damaged section of a seventeenth century Bishop's chair from St Leonard's church in the village of Apethorpe, I was lucky that only one arm of the chair was destroyed, as I had the other to "copy" from. This I did by scratching the profile of the good piece onto a piece of clear acrylic sheet with a scriber, then rubbing oil-paint into the scratches. This gave me an exact profile and scale for the opposite arm.'

Detective meets forger

'In every piece of restoration work there are evaluations to be made and decisions to be reached and agreed with the client, before you pick up a chisel,' explains Glyn. 'You approach the task as a detective and finish it like a forger. It's not only a question of matching the design, style, material, finish and patina, you have to feel your way through the original carving process, put yourself in the same shoes as the original craftsman. There can be a temptation to "improve" on his original concept, but it must be resisted. No matter if he was a better or worse craftsman than yourself. It is he, and not you, who decides on the quality and design of the reproduction, even if he has been dead for centuries.

'Sometimes there is no original work left to copy from, then it is necessary to research similar pieces of a similar period, in libraries and museums, and just extrapolate. It is a strange combination of truth and duplicity.'

Overcoming problems

Working with modern carving gouges can cause problems in restoration and reproduction projects. Although the quality of tools is as good or better now, shapes are different. The original craftsman might have made his own tools or had them made specially for him. Old tools are inclined to be thinner, may have been broken and re-ground, or improved with wear and use. Luckily Glyn recently acquired a collection of 147 chisels dating from 1863-70.

Above **From garden shed to professional studio**
Left **Misericord: a project where the task is reproducing the work of another craftsman**

Photographs by Ron Bull and Glyn Mould

Left **Glyn Mould working on another village sign, in MDF**
Below **One of the many village signs, this is for Eaton Socon, Cambridgeshire**

Suitable materials are also in short supply. Friends are always on the look-out for pieces of timber, either offcuts of new wood or old furniture that can be cannibalised to provide good, well seasoned pieces.

Not quite perfect

Although Glyn says ruefully that he would probably make more money working in a factory, one gets the impression that we would not swap his way of life. Asked what is the worst part of his job, he unhesitatingly replies, 'the paperwork'. He resents the time spent on keeping books, writing letters, sending out quotations and invoices and getting commissions, necessary though these tasks are. In fact as his reputation has grown, most of his work comes from personal recommendations, although he does still advertise, distribute brochures and demonstrate at craft fairs and county shows.

For Glyn the hardest part of the job is working out

Matching a colour and surface patina to something that has developed over centuries of use, polishing and dust is another kind of challenge. Glyn usually gets the colour right with water stains which can be built up in thin washes, although end-grain sometimes has to be re-cut to remove the darker penetration of the stain. He usually finds that a finish of brown French polish can be built up to reproduce both depth of colour and patina.

Client contacts

Of his new work, the village signs are perhaps best known locally: almost every village for miles around boasts a Glyn Mould sign. Commissions usually come from parish councils or groups such as Women's Institutes. He works closely with them to ensure that his design reflects both the historical and modern nature of the village.

Another aspect of Glyn's work is carving presentation trophies. These also call for special skills: an ability to elicit information from the client about the recipient; to research and develop the design; to convince the client that this is exactly what he or she requires; and then, possibly the easiest part, to carve, finish and present the work.

accurate quotations. When it comes to lettering, it is easy to calculate exactly how long a piece of work will take, letter by letter, but with restoration and creative work it is a different problem altogether, usually resulting in a quote that is too low, but which he will be forced to honour. Sadly, says Glyn, too few people realise how much work goes into a piece. He recalls the words of John Ruskin – 'the quality of a work is remembered long after the price has been forgotten'; and Oscar Wilde – they 'know the price of everything and the value of nothing'. ●

During his career Peter Pascoe has held a variety of jobs, from welder to industrial engineer and management services consultant. He began writing in earnest when he retired from his own consultancy business. He contributes regularly to *Practical Craft* and other national magazines, and carves his own puppets for his other career as a children's entertainer

FINDERS KEEPERS

Stan Bullard finds unwanted wood and stores it for sculpture

As a sculptor and printmaker I collect and use a wide range of recycled materials. My house, workshop and shed are piled up with logs, branches and twigs from a variety of trees. Where this wood came from, its storage and future use, will be the thread stringing together this article.

Wood arrives in my hand by several routes. One route is direct field observation, which is what led me into serious wood sculpture. For years I had noticed a tall, dead hawthorn tree leaning at a rakish angle in a farmer's hedge. Finally this tree keeled over after a heavy snow storm, right across a public footpath. Gallantly, I volunteered to clear away the tree, and the farmer willingly agreed.

Totem pole

This tree, which had seasoned in situ, provided material for my first totem pole. *Totem of Loneliness* is an 8ft, 2.5 m tall sculpture with hardly a crack in it, a hard, durable wood with a rich brown colour. Carving this totem enabled me to explore ideas and feelings about loneliness, and how hands, facial expressions and the position of the body can indicate an individual is lonely.

This was one of my first pieces of sculpture, completed about 16 years ago. All the work was carried out with a mallet (made from the same piece of hawthorn as the totem pole), three half round gouges, a v-gouge and two grades of glass paper. The sculpture is still with me, just fitting into my drawing room, to remind me of a different era of my life.

Recommendation is another avenue for finding wood. A friend asked if I had seen the log lying at the bottom of a nearby lake. The lake, which had just been dredged, exposed the trunk of an oak (*Quercus robur*) completely waterlogged, which had been there for many years.

I did not have a chainsaw at the time, so I cut the log into two pieces each about 300lbs, 136 kg, using an axe. As I was alone, the operation took two days and was completed just before the re-flooding of the lake was due to take place.

Enclosed is the sculpture I produced from one of these logs. It is 5ft, 1.5 m tall and 20in, 0.5 m in diameter. A few weeks later, cracks appeared and the log generally opened up. My theme was based on the experience of a prisoner or restrained individual who feels trapped or 'bottled up', so the outside of the log shape represents the feeling of confinement.

Top **Totem of Loneliness**
Left **Enclosed**

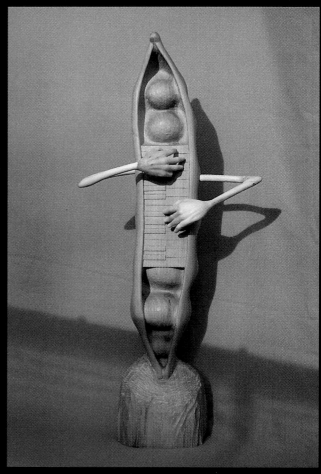

As I worked slowly with just a mallet and gouges, the splitting process seemed to fit exactly with what I had in mind.

Wood storage

A squirrel buries acorns or beechnuts hoping to find them later. But after a few months, he often has difficulty in locating his store. In the past I have found myself in the same situation. It wasn't the nuts, but the oak or beech trunk, stored for several years, I seemed to misplace. I should explain how I manage the wood which comes into my possession.

Seasoned timber from skips or dead trees is stored in a cool, dry shed. Logs are sealed at the cut ends with several coats of wood primer. On this painted area I mark the date of storage and the species of the wood because if the bark falls away after a few years, it may not always be easy to identify.

Drying logs need air circulation and protection from the rain and sun, so I have made a temporary four poster construction with a slate roof cover. I rest the logs on blue brick to protect them from damp and those mini-sculptors, woodlice. As wood seasons slowly in this way (some say at the rate of 1in, 25mm diameter per year), I tend to politely decline offers of 3 ft, 1m diameter logs these days.

I carved a set of musicians from logs stored in this way. Only the *Aubergine Cellist* was different and was carved from a beam rescued during the demolition of a 15th century bell tower.

Friendly offers

Another source of materials comes from friends or acquaintances, clearing sheds and gardens. For those who have no space for storage (and I now belong to this category) here is a very useful tip. When someone offers you a piece of wood, they are likely to have a reasonably large garden, so after explaining that you have no storage space, you could ask them to keep it until you need it. This has worked for me, but you do need to keep a list of which wood lies where, or you might suffer the same fate as the squirrel.

I am often asked where I get my ideas and how I go about realising them in three dimensional form. The answer to this is fairly straightforward, but the methods I use are designed for me and might not suit everybody. Although I employ some of the traditional techniques adopted by craftsmen, there is no need to dwell on them as you can easily find them in print elsewhere.

Here are a few ways I find ideas: The plant musician began as a sketch I had made of a cello playing itself. My friend is a cellist and she is fond of aubergines, so a new concept developed, an aubergine playing itself. After several sketches, I made a small model of the idea in a lovely dark rosewood (*Dalbergia spp*). This helped me to use the 15th century oak beam to its full capacity and I carefully carved it with hand tools, fitting the yew (*Taxus baccata*) arms and legs as I went along.

Cultivating ideas

As I am interested in Man's place in the universe, the musical theme offered some developmental possibilities. Plants are essential to the life of people, I reasoned, so why not explore the idea of people as plants or vice versa? With music as the theme, these ideas began to expand and after some time I had a quartet and even an elder tree conductor.

All these sculptures started as logs and branches, but by far the most delightful of the musicians to work with was the *Tree Flautist*. Made from a fallen branch of a cedar of Lebanon (*Cedrus libani*), the hand-carving of this sculpture filled the whole house with a beautiful scent. I was sorry when it was completed and the wood had to be sealed.

The *Xylophone Mushroom* was made from elm (*Ulmus spp*) and the *Pea-nist* of a resinous softwood. All four musicians stand about 3ft,1m tall. Unfortunately the musicians, like many bands, have separated. Now just one rests with me.

Spontaneous suggestion

Sometimes I work without drawings or preconceived ideas, allowing the wood, my imagination and the chisel to decide the finished article. I carved *War and Peace* from a sycamore (*Acer pseudoplatanus*) branch using this method.

To help me decide on the shape and even its eventual name, I relied on the knots, the rotted section and the grain, always ready to pick up any clues the wood offered. The sycamore responded wonderfully to carving and smoothing, and has retained its silky polished surface, even in its new home in Rome.

Commissions

Another way of working is to be given a commission, such as a dead tree, two weekends and scaffolding to produce a sculpture. This happened to me in June and July 1994, at Normanby Hall Country Park near Scunthorpe in North Kesteven. The tree was 29½ft, 9m tall and 10ft, 3m in diameter at the base and well rooted. I decided to make it a totem pole, with the people and animals of the park as its subject.

I produced lots of quite rough sketches of what I might do with this tree, knowing that as the tree had died there might be some rotting or fungus present. It was a wellingtonia (*Sequoiadendron gigantium*) and I had no previous experience of this type of wood. Because no scaffolding had arrived on the first weekend, I worked from a very solid picnic bench to reach the height I needed. With two weekends to do as much as possible, I had to carve and finish it with a chainsaw.

Opposite top left **Aubergine Cellist**
Opposite top right **Pea-nist**
Opposite bottom left **Tree Flautist**
Opposite bottom right **Mushroom Xylophonist**
Above **War and Peace**

I was one of over 150
sculptors chosen to sculpt
a piece of local wood

Above ***Normanby Totem* at the
end of the second weekend of work**
Right **The Eurosculpture seat**

Imagine my surprise at finding a blood red heartwood rather than a pinkish centre. The wood also had a white fungus between many of the annual rings. So when I cut deeply to form two red foxes in the arms of a figure, the detailed fox sculpture dropped to the ground. What was strange about the lower figure, was a cat-shape which appeared below and despite my efforts, it remained there.

To make good headway with the carving, I decided to camp on the Saturday night and make an early start on Sunday. The loud pop concert that night, and early morning call from what seemed like 99 of the park's 100 peacocks, helped me keep my resolution. At 5.30am I started making tea and spent the day finishing off the lower section of the totem.

On the second weekend, from a tower scaffolding, I sculpted the owl figure at the top of the tree. The pinkish wood was very hard, but in perfect, healthy condition. Working from rough plans rather than from my drawings, I was able to complete the top by the end of the second weekend. Visitors to the park seemed to enjoy watching me, reading my plans and drawings displayed at the bottom of the tree. They were kept outside my safety barrier to escape

falling pieces of wood.

In two weekends I had managed to complete the top and bottom of the totem pole. Two months later the manager of the park wrote asking if I would return in summer 1995 to complete the project. I readily agreed as I had always wanted to carve a dead tree in situ and I wanted to complete the totem pole.

Eurosculpture

Shortly after this project I visited the Eurosculpture event in Carhaix, Brittany (France). I was fortunate to be one of over 150 European sculptors chosen to sculpt a piece of local wood or stone in the huge country park. My piece of wood was situated in a wooded valley between two lovely oaks.

What wood was it? Wellingtonia, a piece 6½ft, 2m tall, 23½in, 60cm in diameter. Although I had prepared a special design for Eurosculpture, I found I had to completely change the project.

When I was sitting on the grass in this lovely valley with chaffinches and goldfinches singing I decided I had to make a seat in which people could listen to the birds. The sculptors were given five days in which to complete their

projects, so with chainsaw, hand adze, mallet and gouge I worked for five days, shielded from the hot sun by the dappled shade of the oaks.

Deep into the heartwood I carved a hollow seating area. Not only could I hear bird song amplified, but my voice took on an echoing quality. I extended the sound theme as the work progressed and the sides of the hollowed log became thinner and thinner. By tapping the walls in different areas, various percussion sounds could be played. It was almost a wooden version of a steel band instrument.

As a design for the outside of the sculpture, I chose to chase around the red knots caused by cut branches. What a marvelleous opportunity and setting. I was able to sculpt, inspired by the environment, where the practical application owed its method and execution to the nature of the wood.

Most of my recent sculptures, like my first hawthorn sculpture, follow the shape of the trunk, and to some extent this shape can be discerned in the finished piece. Trunks, logs and branches provide me with a regular source of sculptural material, while the tree itself holds a fascination for me which spills over into ideas and inspirations for drawing, printmaking and sculpture. ●

Born in Nottingham, Stan Bullard has a rich background of industrial and teaching experience. For the last 10 years he has worked as a sculptor and printmaker from his studio in Beeston, Nottingham. He holds exhibitions and works on residencies, workshops and commissions in Great Britain, France and the Channel Islands. Whenever possible he uses re-cycled materials for his sculptures and believes that we should try to live in harmony with the natural environment.

Lori Freeze discovers why Charles Widmer turned to carving humorous caricatures

ONLY WHEN I LAUGH

Charles Widmer has been carving full-time for more than 25 years. He has crafted an American eagle for former United States President Jimmy Carter and other high profile pieces which have brought him fame, if not fortune. But humorous caricatures which make people smile give him the most satisfaction now.

After many years producing projects to please other people, Widmer is now working to make himself happy. The 48-year-old master carver and his wife, Linda, operate a shop in Mountain View, Arkansas. The shelves are filled with caricatures and scenes depicting Ozark Mountain heritage.

The pieces he likes best are the ones that make people laugh – a hillbilly shotgun wedding, dogs with crooked tails treeing a raccoon, or an elderly couple rushing for an outhouse, for instance. "I get more satisfaction out of that than I ever have from an 'artsy' piece which makes people contemplate or brings a spiritual message," says Widmer.

He was once told by a friend he was making a huge mistake by not continuing production of the large, intricate carvings which could eventually make Widmer famous. But he doesn't regret his move away from producing furniture and free-standing sculptures which involve hundreds, even thousands, of hours work.

Widmer brings to life only those ideas he enjoys carving, a method which has made him a much happier and relaxed person, he said.

"I don't carve to please other people. If a carving sits in the shop for 20 years that's okay, I like it," he comments.

Whittling down

The Widmers have simplified their life by closing the section of their store devoted to other artwork and crafts. They display only carvings and Linda's silver jewellery. The couple live in an adjoining apartment, opening the shop five days a week. Charles carves every day the shop is open, but only during that time so he avoids "burn-out".

"I see people devote too many hours to it. They're the ones who quit. I want to carve as long as I'm physically able to do so," he says.

Unlike some carvers, Widmer works whether or not he is inspired or in the mood. "Art is my business and I approach it as a business," he explains.

Regular routine

His regular work schedule differentiates him from hobby carvers. Even so, there are more ideas in Widmer's head than there are hours to recreate them in wood. "I have so many ideas I'll never get them all carved," he told me.

Nearly every day he thinks of an idea for a carving, developing the basic concept as a picture in his mind. "I think a lot in pictures," he says, "not in words".

Many of his ideas come from people he sees

Left **Medicine Man (1986) – a life-sized head carved in walnut.** Photo by Ed Schuh

Shotgun Wedding in basswood, involved about 100 hours work

around the courthouse square in the rural Ozarks town. As crowds gather to listen to folk music, Widmer scans faces, remembering certain features. "I see people I like and remember a face or a nose and put it into a carving the next day."

Creating caricatures

Widmer's approach to creating caricatures is similar to his favourite artist, Norman Rockwell, who Widmer says could achieve the perfect blend of caricature and realism. "I'm a big Norman Rockwell fan," he says. "I like his way of thinking, of approaching his art."

Widmer believes to do caricatures properly, an artist must understand anatomy. "If you don't understand anatomy, whether it's a dog, horse, or human, your caricature will suffer." For instance without knowledge of a dog's anatomy a caricature can appear to be just a poor carving of a dog. "You can't alter reality to create a caricature until you understand the reality you want to alter. That's where most caricature artists get in trouble."

Widmer lists Bob Robertson of Branson, Missouri, among his mentors. "My work is quite different from his, but I appreciate his dedication to the art of woodcarving." Robertson's work usually carries a western theme featuring cowboys or Indians, while Widmer's is now almost exclusively caricatures with country themes.

Widmer considers the Flemish, German and English carvers (14th–16th centuries) some of the best carvers in the world, creating astonishingly detailed realism. "It's beyond realism, almost every detail is to the extreme of credibility. I've always enjoyed that type of work," he says.

Unlike some carvers, Widmer claims he is not a natural-born artist. "Nothing comes easily to me. I have to think through each process. I work out all the problems as I go, both technically and artistically. It makes my work 'work' but it also keeps me challenged."

Preparation

To help him work through each process, Widmer first sculpts an idea from artists' clay and sketches pencil drawings, techniques common among carvers. "My betters tell me this is the way to do it and I agree. The theory is to make your mistakes in clay. It's a good theory. It works."

"The hardest part for me is the basic structure, not the details," Widmer says during our interview in his shop. He talks while adding bits of clay to a figure which will be a pattern for an Indian series called Winter Wind. The male figure on which Widmer was working was climbing up a rocky slope, turning slightly with one arm reaching back to help a female companion.

The sculpture enables Widmer to become as familiar with the work as he can before he commits himself to wood. This

Uncle Earl is Widmer's favourite uncle. The chair and man are carved from one piece of basswood

process can take three to four days for a 9in, 230mm figure. The bigger the piece, the more time is required for preparation.

Transferring ideas

Time is not a factor Widmer takes into consideration as he carves, although pricing is based on it. "I take whatever time is necessary to get the job done properly," he says. Unfortunately, he adds, finances often pressure some carvers.

He believes if you worry about how long it takes to do a piece, it affects the quality of the work. Widmer has had to adjust the price of pieces which took too long to complete, but he considers it something an artist has to accept.

Transferring an idea from his mind, to paper, clay, and then finally to wood is fundamental to Widmer's theory of woodcarving. Widmer believes works of art are created in the artist's mind, whereas some carvers think the object is locked up in the piece of wood and they release it by carving chips away.

"A block of wood is just a block of wood," he says. "All the thought and feeling and motion comes from the mind, through the hands and into the wood."

ranging in size from ⅜in, 8mm wide x ¹⁄₁₆in, 2mm deep to ¾in, 20mm wide x ¹⁄₁₆, 2mm deep. He also uses a set ranging from ⅜in, 8mm wide x ⅛in, 4mm deep to ¾in, 20mm wide x ¹⁄₁₆in, 4–5mm deep. He has hundreds of tools, though his collection has shrunk from previous years. About 100 are considered his "favourites," including many shallow sweeps.

To rough out his wood initially, Widmer uses a band saw and hand coping saw. For safety's sake, he uses a vice to hold most pieces while he carves.

The basswood figures in this outhouse scene stand 125mm, 5in tall

Tool selection

The knife is Widmer's primary tool. Since his grandfather bought him a pocket knife when he was seven years old, Widmer has always whittled in his spare time, not shying away from the title of whittler, like some carvers.

"I started a whittler, I'm still a whittler and I'll probably always be a whittler," he comments.

A knife with a 1⅛in, 30mm blade is his favourite tool for 9in, 230mm figures, though his workbench holds a selection of gouges, skews and other knives in various sizes.

About 21 tools are kept within easy reach, including many palm gouges (v-shaped and u-shaped), skews from ¹⁄₃₂–¹⁄₁₆in, 1–2 mm to ⅜in, 10mm, and three knives with blades ranging from ⅝in, 15mm to 1in, 25mm long.

His 10 favourite chisels for use with a mallet are mostly u-gouges

Artistic advantage

Widmer has an extra advantage in being ambidextrous, allowing him to use both hands with equal ease. The skill is especially important when carving faces. He achieves a better balance, or symmetry, by carving the right side of the face with his left hand, and vice versa. He says the more you develop this skill, the better your advantage.

Holding a rough-cut shape which is the beginning of one of his hound dogs, Widmer works and chats, changing tools without even realising it. "A lot of what I do is subconscious," he explains. "I'm into the art, and not the nuts and bolts of carving. A number of years ago it was a battle just to know what tool to pick up."

Widmer contemplates the *Anniversairy Couple*. The subtitle is "Me and Pa share everything and today's his day for the denture."

Man and raccoon, carved in basswood

Furniture flair

Despite his ready access to forest areas, good carving wood is hard to find, partly because of its popularity for use in furniture.

Widmer is familiar with popular furniture woods because he devoted around one-third of his career to the craft. For many years he created very detailed furniture in the Old World style using his and Linda's original designs. "The basic piece would be Queen Anne or Chippendale, for instance, and we would add our own flair." They aimed to create something of their own in a proven style.

Their designs tended to be more realistic than the traditional stylised art, and Widmer took them to a higher degree of detail and finish than most carvers.

He never selected top-grade wood for furniture, preferring instead pieces he described as having more character because of their appealing features.

He believed a knot could be cleverly worked into a design and a distinct grain pattern could be used to advantage.

Self motivation

He enjoyed the challenge of matching the grain for a pleasing effect, and never used straight-grained wood for his furniture.

Although he has carved commission pieces such as a life-sized American bald eagle for the Carter Library in Atlanta, Georgia, Widmer is inspired no longer by the prospect of carving for fame or fortune. He carves to make himself, and others, happy.

His advice to other carvers is to be similarly self-motivated. "It's one thing to be the best carver, but to be the best carver you can be is more important." Achieving that goal can be a life-long process. "You won't be the best carver you can be until you've carved your last piece." ●

The tools no longer intimidate him and their use comes naturally.

It took most of his career to achieve that level of confidence, just as it took 20 years to fully understand the various characteristics of wood. "I'm not a fast learner, but I'm persistent," he comments.

He feels artists must develop a mastery of tools and a complete understanding of wood to be successful. It's not until a carver has mastered the use of tools and understands the grain and flow of wood that his art can fully develop. For example, as Widmer continues work on the hound dog he knows at what angles the wood will carve and, without thinking, turns the piece appropriately. "Learning to do that intuitively is important," he says.

Knowing what type of wood will be appropriate is also critical. Widmer uses mostly basswood (*Tilia americana*), black walnut (*Juglans nigra*) or butternut (*Juglans cinerea*). He occasionally uses lime (*Tilia vulgaris*) or sassafras (*Sassafras albidum*), choosing a piece for its particular characteristics.

Basswood is the softest and easiest to work, while black walnut provides a beautiful dark-grained effect and butternut has a unique marbled grain pattern.

Anniversairy Couple, carved in basswood

Lori Freeze is a 30-year-old newspaper editor and freelance writer from Mountain View, Arkansas, USA. Many of her childhood summers were spent roaming the craft grounds of the Ozark Folk Center State Park in Mountain View. She has developed a natural appreciation for the arts and crafts of the area and enjoys writing about them. The woodcarving shop was one of her favourite haunts, and she often tried her hand at carving under the supervision of the master woodcarver there.

AS GOOD

For Tom Langan, being a folk artist means being an unschooled artist. He has not had any formal training in this field, but through diligence and experimentation, he has become part antiquarian, part chemist, part wood technologist, and most of all an outstanding artist. What comes from these ingredients are masterpieces of folk art that range from waterfowl and mythological figures to menageries of felines, foxes, fish and cows, and even caricatures of America's folk heroes.

One of his carvings is a rooster astride a ball-topped newel post. It has the patina of weathered bronze, yet it is only weeks old. Another, a whirligig in the shape of America's most popular symbol, Uncle Sam, has arms which rotate in a feisty manner. Another is a spirited fox.

Tom Langan of Roslyn Harbor, New York, USA is a folk artist who not only makes original compositions but also gives many of his pieces such old patinas the carvings look as if they have survived a century or more. He says he is giving his works a history of their own.

Langan's entry into folk art was stimulated by an interest in duck hunting. Ducks are readily hunted near his home on the water, but waterfowl often need to be lured into shooting range. As a result, decoys are a necessity for

hunters like Langan and he decided to make his own rigs of wooden birds.

When he saw he could carve a decoy and do it well, he found the confidence to market his work. The public accepted his birds and he took the risk of carving folk art for a living. Today he enjoys financial success and recognition in the art world.

Mixing mediums

Although many of his creations are wood sculptures, Langan points out a strong characteristic of folk art is mixing mediums and, he says, a true folk artist will do just that. If, for example, a folk artist of the past was creating a heron, he would find a piece of

AS OLD

Roger Schroeder meets
Tom Langan who specialises
in antique effect folk art

horsehair or leather and make the bird's crest from that.

Carving feathers, Langan says, doesn't give the bird the same type of feeling or movement. When working up his own compositions, he might make tail feathers from copper sheets. The tong of a clam rake will end up as the bill of a curlew.

To give a decoy an antique look, he takes a piece of rusting mending plate and secures the neck to the body with it, after he has nailed the neck in place with old nails. Langan describes many of his pieces as the product of available materials, items a folk artist of old would have found in a barn, basement, or a boat house.

But there is more to his work than rusty additions. He says he feels most comfortable with a piece when it projects a history, a story, a life of its own. "I often make something look older than it really is," he says. "I found it easiest to get that feeling of antiquity by using aged material or making my finishes look as if they have been broken down by time."

....

Top left A fox, 34in, 865mm long
Top right A horse with a bronze patina, 30in, 760mm long
Left A rooster with metal tail feathers, patinated to give a weathered copper look

Old wood

One of the key ingredients in artificially making something look older than it really is, is not so artificial at all. The secret lies in using old wood.

After nearly 20 years as a folk artist, Langan has found some unusual sources of wood, especially wood which looks old. When he was making decoys that looked as if they had some history, he selected wood that old time decoy makers would have used, pine (*Pinus spp.*) and cedar (*Cedrus spp.*).

Near his home were barges which had been submerged for some time. These timbers were yellow pine. Although the wood from the barges was as hard as oak, and as buoyant as a boulder, the timbers had substantial dimensions and he made a variety of birds from them without having to laminate pieces.

Later, he used utility poles. Rectangular in shape, the poles were of solid red cedar (*Thuja plicata*) and used to light roadways that criss-crossed the island he lives on. When the old wood poles were replaced by aluminium ones, they became available to Langan. Other sources have been telephone poles and even old flagpoles, but he still favours the old light poles.

Scorched surface

Langan wasn't satisfied with using wood which may have been around for 50 years. To speed up the ageing process he burned the wood. When he wanted his decoys to look not only old, but well used, he found burning the surface removed wood from between the tell-tale growth rings, resulting in the rings being more prominent. This effect suggested the abuses of handling and weather.

He compares burning to a primitive kind of sanding, but he warns not to use intense heat. Only the surface must be burned, and not all woods burn well, he points out. His barge wood will ignite itself because of its turpentine content, and fir gets too grainy. The best wood he finds for burning is white cedar (*Chamaecyparis thyoides*), though it is not as readily available as red cedar.

Patinas

During his years as a folk artist, Langan has been almost relentless in devising patinas which suggest old age. A decade ago he experimented with finishes which would break down and crack. He discovered he could do this by applying varnish over wood which was not thoroughly dry and then apply layers of oil or lead paint over that. After a while the surface paint would crack.

Langan once said you can't take the paint out of a can and expect it to have an old patina. That is something which will happen in 60 years. But someone suggested he could get that very effect from a spray can. The product is called Krackle, a lacquer-based product, available at many paint stores. As it dries it does just as its name suggests.

Today, Langan has developed still different techniques. What he is looking for now is another kind of finish which has the immediate look of having been broken down by time. What he uses for some of his pieces are plaster of Paris, gesso, and oil paint.

He paints only certain areas with a mix of wet plaster and gesso. Over the dried mix he applies oil paints. Soon the plaster breaks away from the surface, lifting the paint and

He also found it effective to expose a painted piece to the outdoors. "If you had a carved and painted bird outside for two years, very few people could tell its real age," he says. "After five years, I think even the experts would be fooled."

He based many of his experiments on observations of weathered wood. He observed how nature and time changed the material, noting how enamel paint which had been brushed onto the glass surface of storm windows cracked faster than paint on the wood.

He explains the porosity of the wood will let the paint dry smoothly, but on a shiny surface the paint will dry without taking hold the same way. It tends to crack from the harsh effects of sun and water.

Main picture
**A pair of swans in cedar
36in, 915mm long**

exposing the wood. Making wood look porous and old takes days instead of decades.

Yet another patina Langan has worked up is one which gives the look of aged copper or bronze. Once he has sealed the wood with varnish, he applies a metal foil, a faux gold, in a similar manner to a gilder. Putting salt water or bleach on the surface does the job of moving time quickly ahead by producing a greenish patina of age.

Work ethic

Langan spends a minimum of time on each piece, often working on only three or four pieces at a time. In fact, the longest he claims to have spent on a piece of folk art is a week. Most of the carvings are done in half that time.

Above **An Uncle Sam folk art caricature with articulated arms**

He refers to decorative waterfowl carvers who spend hundreds of hours on a carving and ultimately burn out after a few birds. He believes by taking so long, "they're using up money on commissions they haven't even started yet."

"I see a psychological deprivation in that type of work," he says. "The more time you spend with a piece, the more worn out you get and the harder it is to give it up. I don't go into great detail with what I do, so I should be able to make a piece in two or three days. I just don't have the long term dedication."

Market forces

What quickens the production of this work is his attention to themes. "I have moved along with the trends of what is the most marketable, from decoys to animals to people," he explains.

His series of roosters, some patinated to look like copper creations and others polychromed, is one such theme. He spent six weeks on these animals before he moved on to other themes such as snakes, flounders, or political figures.

The latter, he says, are not political statements but merely an attempt to fill a void on the folk art market.

Despite his need to work quickly, Langan does spend time at the drawing board working up new poses and positions for his themes. He will do five or six drawings of a rooster or a fox, though he may reject half of them. What he looks for are different movements or postures. Still, the drawings are basic, with some having more detail than others, and many being just profiles.

Production shortcuts

A decade ago Langan worked on as many as 25 small shore-birds at one time. These days he keeps his production down to six or seven pieces a month. What has helped over the years to produce that number of similar items is a duplicating machine.

Though he rarely uses it now, he states, "I could never have survived as long as I have without using it on occasion. It's a time-saver. And although it may create repetition, you can change each piece to a degree. It does only about 70% of the carving, which means the rest you have to do by hand with some creative changes."

Langan's duplicator and studio are not at his home but at a furniture factory 30 miles away. There, in a setting of massive jointers, bandsaws, and other industrial-grade equipment, Langan gets his work done.

Air tools are also available to him at the factory, and these are indispensable for many operations. Air-powered rotary cutters, sanders and bits remove wood quickly and efficiently. These, too, are the tools of a professional carver.

Langan describes himself as a survivor because he is making folk art at a production level with a system that gets as many as 100 pieces done each year. He says he never saw himself as a romantic who made figures with an axe and drawknife, next to a stove.

However, he does view himself as a professional, one whose work is in the permanent collection of the Museum of American Folk Art in New York City, has been on exhibit at the Smithsonian Institute in Washington, D.C, and has even appeared in an Absolut Vodka promotion. He says he is very satisfied being a folk artist, and expects to continue for many more years. ●

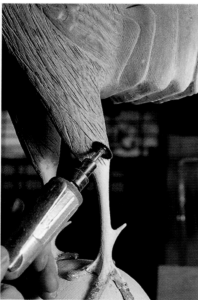

Top **A polychromed rooster in cedar**
Above left **The polychromed rooster before finishing. The tail feathers are cut from a copper sheet and the feet are moulded lead**
Above right **Langan textures the rooster's surface using an airtool handpiece and a rotary saw blade**

Roger Schroeder is a prolific writer and lecturer on woodworking, construction, sculpture and carving, as well as a cabinet-maker and amateur carver. He combines these activities with a full-time job as a high school English teacher, specialising in teaching creative writing and research.

Benoi Deschênes discusses Pier Cloutier's profound influence on Québec's cultural heritage and artistic future

LIVING LEGACY

With plenty of talent and abundant creativity, painter and sculptor Pier Cloutier easily found his place in a bastion of devoted sculptors in 1960s Québec.

Well-directed, sensitive to his art and its trends, this artist knew how to embark upon all his prospective achievements. He was a staunch supporter of freedom of expression, which he defended when confrontations arose between the establishment and the new wave of freethinkers.

Self-taught and independent in the field of research, Pier explored Europe through the museums of Paris, Barcelona, Rome, Athens and Milan. Since he was quite tall and thin, giving the appearance of frailty, this man astonished many with the strong and courageous style present in each of his accomplishments.

Above **Pier Cloutier at work on** *Untitled*

Right *Dame Blanche*, **the subject of an article published by the National Geographic Magazine**

Far right **The door of Pier Cloutier's home, sculpted in pine and representing the spirits of 12 worldly scholars responsible for the advancement of man**

In 1975 the Musée des Anciens Canadiens in Saint-Jean Port-Joli, Québec opened their doors to him by commissioning a collection of work still displayed today, a precedent of the period. As he had only a few years' experience and a limited supply of knowledge, this showed great faith in his skills.

Serene sculpture

As well as many other pieces, he produced *La Femme Au Chapeau* (Lady In A Hat), a life-sized sculpture carved from one block of pine (*Pinus spp*) which became the masterpiece of the museum.

His wife served as a model while Pier fashioned the body with explicit accuracy and respect for each detail of her garments, such as the straw hat worn for protection against the summer sun. When viewing this piece, you sense a feeling of quiet reflection and fluidity of movement. A true message of serenity is transmitted by the crossed arms and folded hands of the sculpture.

Pier was not diverted by the public's applause and critics' flattery. He continued to devote time daily to further exploration of his craft. He wrote a book in which the art of engraving was combined with sleek woven wall-coverings. Travelling further along the journalistic path, *National Geographic* magazine published an article about his sculpture entitled *Dame Blanche* (*White Lady*).

Three symbols

In 1984 Pier participated in the International Sculpture Symposium in Saint-Jean Port-Joli where he created one of his most monumental productions. *A Triptych* consisted of three large rectangular panels measuring approximately 4 x 2m, 13 x 6½ft, which were sculpted in wood and then cast in aluminium.

This collection represents three styles of writing by different civilizations. The first style is the native writing of symbols and characters on animal skins placed in a sacred site. The second represents unfolded organic paper showing a sensitivity for ecology. The third style is about computer technology and the distinction of modern times. The three panels, permanently installed on the artist's property, are mounted on poles and vibrate with the wind.

Left **Untitled, shows his sensitivity to art**
Below **A Triptych represents three styles of writing by different civilisations**

even under the best conditions.

Determined to make it work, however, I pressed on all the same. Today, the fitting of this sculpture brings me back to the time of Pier Cloutier and the memory of him, for the last time, greeting me with a wave of his hand and that gentle, disarming smile.

Next generation

Pier had a great influence on the young sculptors of his generation by encouraging them to go further artistically than they had previously thought possible. This work has been continued by the Pier Cloutier Foundation which was started in 1991, with the purpose of aiding artists.

The funding has been made possible partly by the sale of 10 bronze copies of Pier's work *Le Couple*, and 275 lithographic reproductions of one of his paintings entitled *La Solitude*. My thanks to Marthe Castonguay, his widow, and to the Musée des Anciens Canadiens for their valuable contributions. ●

Dark day

Pier and I always had peaceful and absorbing conversations. Working in the same field, we held a mutual respect for one another, which allowed amicable artistic exchanges.

In 1985 Pier, barely 40 years old and fighting a brain tumour, quietly slipped away with his wife Marthe, and daughter Isabelle by his side. It was March and the heavy rain and sleet pounded our homes as well as electric cable poles. Most of Québec was plunged into a black-out which lasted several days.

During this time I was forced to glue pieces of ash-walnut (*Juglans spp*) together for a sculpture I was creating, by the light supplied by car batteries. The varying tints of this wood are quite difficult to arrange and hard to work

Benoi Deschênes is one of Canada's most noted woodcarvers. He studied sculpture at Jean Bourgault's school in St-Jean Port-Joli where he now resides and has his studio. Subsequently he studied visual arts in Cap Rouge under the guidance of painter Arthur Côté. A professor of arts, Benoi spent five years teaching at Saint-Pamphile and L'Islet-sur-Mer, Québec, and was created laureate of woodcarving in 1978.

Zoë Gertner carves a wide variety of subjects in her own particular style.

Zoë Gertner is a professional woodcarver and teacher, she has taught woodcarving to people aged from 8 to 85 years old, including the inmates of one of Her Majesty's establishments. Zoë works by commission and these have included a proscenium for a fairground organ, a pair of 5ft long swans for a roundabout, as well as a few pew ends in Wedmore church, Somerset. Zoë Gertner has exhibited her carvings widely, and her work can be found in collections all over the world.

My *Somerset Applepicker*, made from a single piece of yew, is about 14in high. I carved this because someone said it would not be possible to carve a tree in the round, from a single piece of wood. Through lack of choice, I used a very freshly cut section, split from a log I had acquired, which actually

Somerset Applepicker, in yew, about 14in high

spurted water when the endgrain was cut. Hollowing out and excavating between the branches very successfully relieved the stresses which might have produced cracks

smooth surface, which I then wax again and buff up with a lint-free duster. I also scrape the surfaces to be tooled, because it is impossible to tool or texture cleanly on a poor quality base.

Baskets and boxes

Having seen the baskets I carve, someone asked me to make one for her daughter containing two kittens, one of which had to be lying on its back with its feet in the air. I used a section of yew so that the sapwood could be utilised as the wickerwork, and the heartwood as colour contrast for the animals. The carving is from one piece, including the knitting needles. A sample square of knitting for me to copy was provided by an obliging student of mine, since my skills do not include knitting. The wool is wound round the kitten's foot. When I carved the unsupported strand of wool, I reinforced the cross-grain with glue to strengthen it, and supported it from underneath with a ball of plasticine.

A selection of boxes, each carved, including the hinge and catch, from a single piece of wood. The first style I devised was round, taken from a cross-section of a log, so that with woods such as plum I can make use of the colour contrast between the heart and sapwoods. The chest style caskets are made

PERSONAL

and splits as the wood dried out. The front of the man on the ladder had to be carved through the rungs, the ladder being carved first with a block left attached to it to allow for the figure. It is finished with wax polish, as are most of my carvings.

I like to make full use of the contrast, not only in colour between the heart and sapwood, but also by using textures. The doves are carved from yew, mainly smooth, with a little tooling on the base for added tactile as well as visual interest. To achieve a really fine smooth finish, I scrape the surfaces, then apply a coat of cheap polish, leave it a little while to soak in, then abrade the surface with 320 grit garnet paper. The abraded dust mixes with the polish, and fills the pores of the wood, to give a very fine

Doves, in yew taking advantage of the contrast in colour between heart and sapwood

from lime, mainly because it is quick and easy to carve. The 'prototype' first one I made was the basket of doves, which fly out towards you when the lid is lifted, the birds being carved from inside the lid. Having worked out the hingeing system, I then developed integral catches to fasten their lids, and carved different creatures inside each box.

One Spring day I walked down the road with the dog, and saw a group of sheep with their lambs, one of which was perched on the back of its mother, and I thought this would make a good carving. To my pleasure, shortly afterwards I was asked by someone if I would make her such a group for an anniversary present, preferably in apple wood. This carving was my second attempt, due to an annoying unrectifiable arrow-shaped bark pocket (to which apple is

Sheep with a lamb, in apple wood, about 8in long

rather prone) revealing itself between two of the sheep; it grew larger the more I carved. The carving is about 8in long, and the wool is textured using a deep U-shaped gouge wiggled and twisted to follow the lie of the wool.

One of a pair of 'brothers', which I originally started for a demonstration at Yandles Autumn Exhibition. In lime wood, about 8in high, he has been at the cider jar, discarded his sandals, and lost two of the three knots on his cord belt, which represent the vows of poverty, chastity and obedience. His robe is hollowed out underneath, though he still wears his long johns.

The second 'brother' has caught his foot in his robe, and is tripping. Dressed like the first one with long johns, his robe is also hollowed, but supported by the higher foot, he is also about 8in and carved from lime wood.

Boxes carved from the solid, including hinges and in some the catches

RESENTATION

Kittens in a basket, in yew

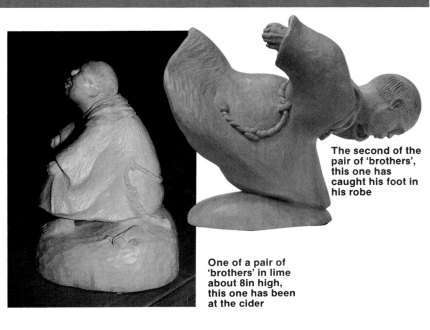

The second of the pair of 'brothers', this one has caught his foot in his robe

One of a pair of 'brothers' in lime about 8in high, this one has been at the cider

A great tit on a string of nuts, cherry, about 11in long

Becoming short of shelf space, I decided to try a hanging carving, again a small bird, this time a great tit on a string of nuts. The bird is attached at four places, feet, tail and beak, and the whole piece is carved from a single length of cherry wood, about 11in long. I use carver's chops for holding such delicate pieces, as they give more access than other holding methods.

The night before Christmas, in cherry about 3in high

The Night Before Christmas. This was taken from the well known verse of the same name, and carved in cherry wood, about 3in thick. The verse is written on the page using a heated point — I filed the tip of a soldering iron to a fine point. The space between the pages and the holly leaves is hollowed right through.

Small birds

A carved small bird needs to be distinctive, so that one can tell what species it is, and for this commission a robin was specified. Robins are well known for nesting in strange places, so it seemed appropriate to place the nest inside an empty plant pot, particularly as the recipient is a keen gardener. It is carved from one piece of lime about 7in, with ivy leaves around the pot.

Feathers carved as an exercise in gouge control

Feathers and hens

Feathers, carved as an experiment to see how finely I could go — it is almost possible to see through these, carved from a sliver of apple wood. Though it would have been possible to grind the poor things into shape using rotary burrs, I avoided the noise and dust and used gouges only; mainly as an exercise in tool control, much as a musician practises scales. I carved one in yew wood, using the heartwood for the shaft and the sapwood for the rest, as a colour contrast.

Hen on a milk churn, from a 2in diameter branch of yew, the nest in sapwood

A robin with its nest in a plant pot

Hen on a Milk Churn. This was carved from a small branch of yew, about 2in diameter, using the sapwood for the straw of the nest. The straw was textured using a v-tool, and the carving stands about 3in high. ∎

Robert Jakes explains
how his large scale sculptures
are influenced by their surroundings

I try to be resourceful, making use of materials which have been cast out. When storms hit the South East of England in the 1980s, I was surrounded (as well as being almost crushed while driving) by fallen trees. Overnight an incredible resource had appeared. Most people just wanted the trees out of the way and were only too pleased if I could help. I began to realise the rich tradition and wealth of imagery available through woodcarving.

The timber being unseasoned, and large scale, prompted me to work outside, often carving the tree on the site where it had fallen.

Red Arrows and Greenhouse (12ft 6in, 3.8m tall) was carved from the crown of a fallen oak (*Quercus robur*). The image of a glasshouse with inlaid mirror appears in quite a number of my sculptures of this period. It generally represents a fragile environment and specifically my glasshouse at home which was destroyed by a large bough.

Working on this scale, I used a Husqvarna 254 petrol chainsaw and completed the small details by hand. The potential of the chainsaw led me to try more detailed work such as *Tumblin' Dice*, carved from a single piece of storm-felled chestnut (*Aesculus hippocastanum*), and *The Tree of Knowledge* where minimal hand carving was involved.

This led on to more detailed hand carved works such as *Battleship/Tableware* and *Bigshirt*, where I wanted to work in the tradition of the medieval painted carvings which depict sculpturally exciting everyday objects as having a symbolic meaning.

Battleship/Tableware was carved from a single piece of oak 8ft 6in, 2.6m long. I made the willow pattern by pasting on photocopies. *Bigshirt* was carved from lime (*Tilia vulgaris*) and beech (*Fagus sylvatica*) 11ft 3in, 3.4m across.

This piece is in the collection of The Grampian Hospitals Art Project and I made it for Aberdeen Hospital during an International Woodcarving Symposium held at The Scottish Sculpture Workshop. It is a direct response to the landscape's hills and valleys, caves and tunnels and it is possible to crawl inside and poke your head out of the collar.

Top **Red Arrows and Greenhouse**
Centre **Tumblin' Dice**
Right **Battleship/Tableware**

LAND MARKS

Schools and symposia

Working alongside woodcarvers from other countries is an exciting and inspiring experience. In 1989, I attended the Monumental Woodcarving Symposium in Hungary and was inspired by its strong tradition of carving. Being surrounded with examples of work in all the public places excites a general feeling of respect from everyone for the skills involved, and this high regard for creative activity is common to all the international symposia I have attended so far.

For many years I have been involved in The Artist in Residence Scheme working in schools with the students to create carved features. At Scarborough 6th Form College we worked for two weeks on the *Gates of Paradise*. This was carved from elm (*Ulmus spp*) in five sections, and is now a permanent feature at the entrance to the Creative Arts Department of the college.

At Brockenhurst College in the New Forest, we worked for just one week carving a 23ft, 7m tall storm-felled Indian cedar (*Toona australis*) which was then re-erected on it's original site. Two days of this time was spent in rigorous discussion about the imagery to be depicted.

Above **The Table**

Left **Robert Jakes works on** *The Tree of Knowledge*
Above ***Totem* at Brockenhurst College**
Below ***Like Leaves From The Trees*, Radford University, West Virginia**

Site specific

My most satisfying work has been creating permanent site-specific pieces for sculpture trails, such as *The Table*, at The Chiltern Sculpture Trail near Oxford. Carved and constructed from storm-felled oak and beech, it was cut to size with a mobile Wood-Miser bandsaw and stands 8ft, 2.4m tall. It acts as a shelter as well as a viewing platform from which to see the surrounding forest from a new point of view.

The decision to build a larger than life table relates to the function of the man-made woodland in which it is situated. The timber is grown to be harvested and consumed while the giant's table sits patiently set for dinner awaiting this day. This image will be all the more poignant when surrounded by the stumps of what has previously been forest.

In all my work I attempt to create pieces which relate specifically to the situations in which they are to be viewed. With the work for Radford University in West Virginia, USA, the main feature was the stunning colours of the maples (*Acer spp*), coupled with the experience of working on the campus. This led to the carving *Like Leaves From The Trees*.

Juxtaposing the two images of a red maple leaf and a giant envelope was a way of playing with words and commenting on the importance of letters, for myself and the many students who had moved onto the campus.

It was constructed from four 6ft, 1.8m long beams of red and white America oak (*Quercus spp*), dowelled together and carved using an electric chainsaw and gouges ranging from No.7 (2in, 50mm), No.4 (1½in, 38mm), No.39 (⅝in, 15mm) V tool and a No.10 (½in, 13mm).

I now live close to the sea in South Pembrokeshire where trees are not as plentiful as in the my previous home of Hampshire. However, the sections of holm oak which have come my way so far have been a very interesting challenge. I have been involved in a race against time carving a cider press, while watching the apples ripen on the trees around me. ●

Robert Jakes was born in Hythe, Kent in 1959. He completed his honours degree in Fine Art at Bath Academy of Art, Corsham in 1981. He has worked extensively in schools and day centres on woodcarving projects and has exhibited his carvings in both group and solo shows, in the UK and abroad. He has a particular interest in making pieces for specific places, and has attended international woodcarving symposia in Hungary, Poland, Italy and the USA. You can contact Richard Jakes at 1 Home Farm Cottage, Stackpole, Pembroke, Dyfed, Wales SA71 5DQ.

FEATURE

BIG
IS BEAUTIFUL

I came to woodcarving from a sculptor's background, so my main aim is to work quickly to produce large outdoor, or structurally proportioned pieces. Although I do work on a smaller scale, especially if commissioned, my real ambition is to make large scale sculptures. Wood is an excellent material to work with on this type of project. It is available in large sizes at a relatively low cost, giving you the opportunity to work with an immediacy that other materials do not necessarily offer. There are also fine traditions to draw upon, from the monumental totems of North America, the Pacific Islands and Asia to the intricate European and stylised African carvings, providing you with a limitless choice of influences and a lifetime's education in the craft.

My first chance to start woodcarving was in 1986 when I was involved with the Bristol Sculpture Shed studios. We developed a large warehouse into workshops for making large scale work. That year we were lucky to be chosen by the Czech artist Magdelena Jetlova, to make her 30 ft, 9m high oak chair at our studios, for the first Forest of Dean Sculpture Trail. The finished chair was then taken back to the forest and can now be seen towering over the valley near Coleford. This project left us with a surplus of large oak logs, and I took the opportunity to try some carving, starting with a life-size figure of a man which I carved entirely by hand.

I soon bought a chainsaw to speed things up. I have not found a better one than the 16 in, 405mm Stihl 024. It is fairly light and responsive but quite powerful and also has the advantage of an extensive nationwide spares and service network. I also have a Sachs Dolmar 109 with a 24 in, 610mm blade for heavy cutting.

Trevor Roberts carves
large scale sculptures from
unseasoned wood

Sourcing materials

I have continued to use unseasoned wood for most of my work. This has the advantage of being relatively cheap or free, with transport and lifting costs being the main financial outlay. The Council Parks Department are usually more than willing to provide local sculptors with materials (the logs I use are often too short, thin, bent or knotted for planking up). They also come from private and sub-contract foresters and tree surgeons, and any other sources that I have built up through my contacts over the years, especially people with gardens or even small woods that need some clearing done.

Splits aid seasoning

The problems of using unseasoned wood are various and often mean having to work with whatever shape and type is available. A common problem is that the wood splits as it dries out. This varies, according to how quickly it dries and what sort of wood it is.

Making large carvings often means the splits do not matter so much and can be filled. They can even be an advantage, enhancing the look of the piece by making it look ready aged. Seasoning supposedly takes one inch per year for each surface, so a 24 in, 610mm diameter log will take 12 years to season. Unless you have foresight and a suitable piece of land, or are willing to rent someone else's, this is not an option for the inspired sculptor.

Which wood

It is tricky to say which unseasoned woods to avoid because different carvings can utilise each type of wood's characteristics. One to avoid is unseasoned beech (*Fagus sylvatica*), as it does split and rot quickly outside. Lime (*Tilia vulgaris*) is a favourite of many carvers as it is soft, although the surface is difficult to get smooth and the grain very subtle.

There is a lot of diseased elm (*Ulmus spp*) available at the moment – very handy for today's woodcarvers as the beetle that carries Dutch elm disease only attacks the bark and outer layers. It is a lovely tight-grained wood to carve

Left **Brighton Belle**, 1993. Lime with metal weathervane. 10ft 6in, 3.2m high.
This carving shows the main essentials of Brighton seaside life. A tourist carries an umbrella in her bag and the weather vane sports a seagull. The pillar is taken from the registry office in the town centre, and is representative of some of Brighton's architectural details, noticed recently when I was married there. It is carved from one piece of lime, and despite being on show outside for several months has kept its colour and surface.

Right **Fume**, 1991. Lime, 6ft, 1.8m high.
This piece is about pollution and ecology, using my style of grotesque figures to give an uneasy humour to the subject. I often use some other materials in my carvings and this is a more extreme example. I have used toy cars and a car's wheel for the base, and a small automata is built into the depictions of chimneys and sewers near the top. The globe, bought from a local newsagent, lights up with the power cable running down through the carving. This is also a rare example of an attempt to colour the wood which was quite plain when first carved. I used washes of oil paint and then lightly sanded the surface to bring out the details.

and holds together well, although varieties differ in their liability to split and the straightness of the grain. Oak (*Quercus spp*) is durable and will last well outdoors with the minimum of preservative, as its hardness and weight suggest. Fruit woods, cherry (*Prunus spp*), pear (*Pyrus communis*), apple (*Malus sylvestris*) etc, are similarly useful and have good grain pattern.

Steps to sculpture

Sometimes I feel confident enough to start carving with only the minimum of sketches. However, as a rule, I develop these into measured drawings, generally a front and a side view, and a maquette or scale model, in clay. Making a maquette gives me the advantage of getting a feel for the three-dimensional quality of the finished sculpture and also brings out any shapes that are not apparent in the two drawings.

As I usually work on a fairly large scale, I start with the log lying on the ground and roll it so I can judge where the front of the log is to be – the aim is to try to avoid knots or holes, or to allow me to use branches or bulges. Having laid the log face up, I measure out and draw (in chalk or emulsion paint) the rough shape taken from the front view drawing. Next, I use the chainsaw to cut off the waste from each side. Then I turn the log 90° and do the same with the profile. This process is repeated on each side, gradually bringing out very square-looking figures. Finally, I start to round off and cut out any holes until I feel I can go no further without risking a mistake.

Next, I start working with my larger 2½in, 63mm and 1½in, 38mm gouges and chisels. I usually like to work on the sculpture in 2 or 3 goes, the first time to rough out the figures and objects, bringing out the general shape and roundness and to discover any problems of knots and splits. Then I go over the piece again bringing out details and character.

Over the years I have built up quite a range of chisels and gouges, usually bought in second-hand tool shops, and have recently started to appreciate the value of having a whole range of shapes and sizes to help speed up work on a variety of details; V shapes for making grooves and emphasising different objects, U shapes for cutting deeper channels and flatter gouges for creating different surfaces.

Fireplace, 1994. Pitch pine 40 x 40 in. 1015 x 1015mm.
I made this for my own house in Brighton, using some 9in, 230mm square beams that a neighbour rescued for me from a building that was having the timbers replaced with steel. The figures represent myself and my wife with parts of our lives strewn around us. It will finally be fixed into place with a metal plate cut to fit inside and around the fire itself. Pitch pine is a lovely wood to carve, with a hard and emphasised grain. There are many old houses in Britain that had beams made from this imported timber, so it is worth looking out for. The splits and nail holes will be filled and coloured with oil paints to match the colour of the wood, and a coating of Danish oil is excellent for bringing out the colour of the wood.

Finishing touches

To finish off I like to use power sanding tools where a chiselled finish is not appropriate. I have flap sanding wheels and discs attached to a drill, but my favourite tool is a Black & Decker power-file sander. It has a ½in, 13mm belt mounted on a small 'finger' that allows me to reach into nooks and crannies as well as being powerful enough to produce certain details and clean edges. Any jointing is usually done using a one inch broom handle stuck into holes in either piece using Cascamite resin adhesive.

There seem to be infinite varieties of finishes for wood, although I try to avoid any that leave a surface layer such as varnish, some wood preservers or even beeswax. Linseed oil and Danish oil help to seal the wood and bring out any grain. For outside pieces maybe Cuprinol five star or Creosote may temporarily look bad but they soak in after a few weeks. ●

Trevor Roberts completed his Fine Art degree at Coventry Polytechnic in 1983. He has since gained a City and Guilds Further and Adult Education Certificate and has been exhibiting his work since 1982. He is also a founder member of the Bristol Sculpture Shed and belongs to the Semi-Ambulant performance arts group. Trevor has exhibited at the Staats Lieden Greep Festival in Amsterdam and a variety of locations in the British Isles, from Brighton to Inverness.

Harriet Hodges is a some-times college English teacher, and a maker of Windsor chairs. She learned the finer points of that craft from Curtis Buchanan. She and her husband live on a Craig County, Virginia, USA, farm and raise sheep in between bouts of dragging in logs for the chairs. She has an exaggerated respect for carving, born of her own struggles with it.

'Kids!' table: the ice cream is walnut and maple. Dimensions 36" W x 18" D x 30" H

Jake Cres

THE FUNNY FURNITURE OF JAKE CRESS

HARRIET HODGES

All is not quite what it seems in Jake Cress' house in Fincastle, Virginia, USA.

The house looks normal enough: a dignified old brick colonial set almost on the edge of a narrow street of one of western Virginia's prettiest little towns. The first-time visitor, entering through the kitchen, is immediately thrown a touch off balance by a blue-fronted Amazon parrot who greets one pleasantly, 'Hello, there.' Difficult to repress the dutiful: 'How are you?' while the eyes search the room wildly for a third person, although clearly one is facing only Jake and his wife Phebe. Getting on with polite conversation, responding to human queries only, one's hand strays idly to the surface of the little table against the wall. A child has stuck a band-aid on it. Sacrilege. The table so beautifully finished. French polished? In the midst of chitchat: '... built in the early 1800s ... shop is a 1784 log cabin ...' the exploring fingers urgently request the eyes to check this bandaid. At the first

Highboy: mahogany

chance, the visitor stares. That bandaid: it's carved it's integral. A maple bandaid on a walnut top. This is 'funny furniture,' furniture with a sly sense of humour that Jake produces along with his pieces of more sombre mien.

Jake enjoys directing the tour from there. The 47-year-old cabinetmaker-carver of 'Furniture Forgeries' has a theatrical flair himself, and it's welcome by. He was several years a radio announcer Later, plunging into acting, he actually supported himself at it for two years. But in 1974 he and a brother decided to be cabinetmakers, hanging the shingle first to learn the craft after. Well after. When they began, they had to manoeuvre a wood dealer into indicating to them which was the walnut. They didn't know. Asked how he learned carving, he says, 'I ruined a lot of good wood'.

Self-taught

The partnership dissolved, but Jake persisted

'Peel Here':
walnut, boxwood.
Dimensions
18" W x 18" D
x 27" H

Entirely self-taught — or instructed by the 18th-Century masters whose work he soon began to repair and restore — his own work is now astonishingly competent. An error in purchasing attests to that. Like most artisans, he buys good old pieces when he can. The kitchen sports a little panelled wall cabinet that Jake relates being instantly drawn to in a dimly lit antique shop. 'When I got it home,' he says with a laugh, 'I looked at it more closely and found it was one I'd made.'

The Cress house, with its rooms of large windows and high ceilings, is the perfect showcase for his own highboys, desk-tables, and frame-and-panelled cabinets. It is also a gallery, exhibiting Phebe's lamps as well as the works of local printmakers and painters. The highboy in the parlour, with its finely carved shell motifs, transmits a museum-like glow from many coats of well-rubbed linseed oil. In the hall are two little tables, a matched set with vines climbing the right leg of one, the left leg of another. They are personality pieces, not exactly 'funny' but still making strong emotional claims. One would hate to see them parted.

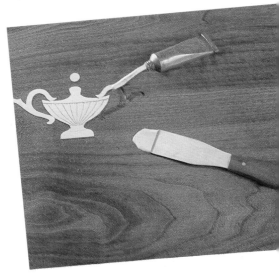

Tube of stuff table: tube is cherry, inlay stuff is boxwood, knife handle is mahogany, blade is brass

'Oops!' table (ball rolling):
mahogany.
Dimensions
36" W x 18" D x
30" L

Laughter

On display are several exquisite handled boxes. One is a miniature sea-chest with tapered sides and angled dovetails ('the hardest thing I ever did,' says Jake). But amidst this decorum, laughter breaks out. On the floor is a little box with a section of its lid 'peeled' back revealing graffiti. And here's a table with a half-finished inlay . . . what's that? He's been squeezing inlay into the groove from a tube? Good lord, hadn't he better finish up here and put that knife away before the stuff . . . One's finger can't help touching. It's carved. Jake laughs, his eyes crinkling gleefully over his half glasses.

Because as good as he is, as finely skilled as he has become, he can't take it too seriously. Or, not all the time. Or perhaps he is so serious that he

labours to make his commentary skilful also. We discuss the movement in the 1980s wherein the maker desecrated his own fine pieces with nails and chalk, to make a statement about pretentiousness, to forestall awe. That unease with perfected craftsmanship is still very much with us. While perhaps our mockery of skill is not as blatant as a nail hammered into a well-fitted panel, we still put perfectionists on the defensive. Jake is not pretentious. He takes his furniture seriously — but his humour also. His ice-cream bars affixed to tables are light-hearted finely-crafted additions, not acts of vandalism.

He would like us to smile. Upstairs, where mayhem reigns, anyone would. Here is his little table with its ball-and-claw feet, one reaching for the ball escaped its clutch. And opposite this

'How to Build
Furniture' table:
one walnut, one
cherry. Same
dimensions 18" W
x 18" D x 27" L

Crutch table:
cherry; tip is
boxwood.
Dimensions
42" W x 18" D x
30" L

Rat-leg table with
sword: mahogany;
sword, cherry.
Dimensions
36" W x 18" D
x 30" L

drama a rat scurries up a table leg, only to be skewered in a most dreadful way by a sword thrust through the tabletop. In this same manic mode is a table now owned by a diplomat, one with a book shoved under a too-short leg, its title reading *How to Build Furniture*. The table with the crutch also belongs to this ménage, but it has been removed to a quiet location by a purchaser that it may recover in peace.

Inspiration

We exit the house for the shop. Everything is straightforward here. Lathe, sander, tablesaw, jointer, and so on. There are no racks of graduated carving tools. 'I use what I have,' he says. And what he has isn't much: a sloyd craft knife, a few chisels, and one gently curved gouge is all he can find in one minute's rummaging. This is real inspiration for me, an aspiring carver, although I hate to give up those wonderful sets I've assembled in my head. Jake does his mouldings by hand — or almost — correcting tablesawn rough-outs with his own filed scrapers. A highboy is nearly finished, its quarter columns fluted, not carved. 'I'd like to do more carving,' he shrugs, 'but people just won't pay for it. They won't give me the week's work it would take here.'

The 'funny furniture' is small. No humour creeps over into the highboys. Clearly Jake feels what makes us smile in a little piece, a small table or a box, is completely inappropriate for a monumental construction and would shortly make us wince instead. He works on the humorous stuff in between the classical, choosing mostly walnut, cherry, mahogany with maple and boxwood for accent. He enjoys the fact that his log-cabin shop was 40 years another woodworker's before he bought it. The shop is two steps off the kitchen door to the fine main house, and in that two steps are 100 years of American history: from log walls to columned fireplaces. Jake's furniture fits with the most formal wainscoting. But if you'd like a small piece to wink at you from a corner, a smile in wood, try carving a walnut joke. ∎

Dr Who, famous Time Lord from the long-running TV series, Australian white beech, 16in, 400mm high. 'I think I took the wood to the limit with the very thin hat brim'

CHARACTER WITNESSES

Thirty years as a policeman gave Don Powell plenty of contact with people, and plenty of inspiration for his subsequent career as a carver

Although born in England, I came to Australia at the age of 11. As a teenager I had been interested in carving and made small animals in walnut, maple and pine using a penknife and a scalpel. However I joined the Queensland Police Force as a young man and woodcarving had to be put aside for a hectic career, and helping my wife Maureen raise five children.

About a year before I left the force I spent several months travelling in Britain and Europe, studying the works of great sculptors, a lifelong interest. On my return I determined to master the craft of carving, and after two years of teaching myself I was fortunate enough to do a three-day workshop with woodsculptor Ian Norbury. This gave me great impetus and I have been working steadily since then: I have now established a good workshop and teach others at college.

All types of carving interest me, but particularly figure carving, of both real people from everyday life, and real and imaginary historical characters. Others have commented that my police career probably influenced my interest in people. It did in fact involve a considerable amount of rubbing shoulders with famous and infamous, rich and poor, working in VIP protection, as Chief Hostage Negotiator and finally in charge of the Witness Protection Programme.

'Maureen, my wife. 12in, 300mm high, carved in marare, a North Queensland rainforest timber similar to rosewood. It was pale pink "in the raw" but once it had been sanded, oiled and buffed with wax it turned dramatically dark, like bronze. I worked from life, and from photographs, but still don't feel I have done her justice'

'A photograph in the Dublin Museum of a potato picker at the turn of the century inspired this piece. She is carved in Queensland walnut and is 14in, 350mm high, finely sanded, oiled and waxed. The mount is a piece of gidgee, an outback scrub timber, on a larger piece of polished teak'

Don Powell

In Australia, carving is not as widespread as it is in England and the US, but it is growing

As a result I met an incredible variety of characters and developed an eye for detail.

In Australia, carving is not as widespread as in England and the US, but it is growing. Ornamental carving for furniture seems to be the most popular style at the moment. Most carvers use Australian white beech (*Gmelina leichhardtii*) which carves easily and cleanly and holds detail well. Camphor laurel, red cedar (*Toona australis*), mango, jacaranda (*Jacaranda mimosifolia*), silky oak (*Cardwellia sublimis*) and avocado are all popular and carve reasonably well.

I have often used lime (*Tilia* spp), rosewood (*Dalbergia* spp) and Queensland walnut (*Endiandra palmerstonii*). I acquired some of this from a furniture maker who used it for billiard table legs. It is harder than European walnut (*Juglans regia*) and is usually avoided by cabinetmakers because it is full of silica and notorious for blunting tools, but I find it carves well.

Many of the timbers from elsewhere in the Pacific region such as New Guinea rosewood, Fijian mahogany and rosewood from the Solomon Islands are growing more popular as they become more readily available.

I prefer to carve with chisels and knives, and love using fine old tools, but have also felt the need to master all the power tools available to achieve the results I want. ∎

***The Image Seller**, 24in, 600mm high, lime and boxwood (**Buxus semper-virens**). 'Inspired by a painting in the Victoria and Albert Museum in London, of a man selling clay figurines. I added the woman and the boy'*

***The Goldpanner**, 14in, 350mm high, Australian white beech, finished with linseed oil, tung oil and waxed. 'This is based on an original photograph seen in a restaurant. I had my son dress up in similar clothes and pose for a photo session to provide reference material'*

A PUBLIC DEBUT

Richard Caink's first commissions have been for public places and play areas

The several years I spent working in forestry and as a tree surgeon gave me invaluable experience for my later incarnation as a woodcarver. Ironically, in all that time I never carved anything, despite having access to a steady supply of timber, and the means to move it around. One of the main problems I now face is getting hold of and transporting decent timber.

I first started my art training after feeling the need to have a career change; I left my job in Cambridge and travelled in France for a while before taking A level art classes and finally a full-time foundation course in art. Sculpture seemed to click with me and the obvious material was wood. I discovered the work of David Nash and other artists carving rough and raw pieces and often sitting them outdoors, particularly in forests – I realised that this is what I wanted to do.

The degree course at Newcastle Polytechnic was a wonderful opportunity to explore sculpture. Although I found the course quite conceptual, I had experienced the importance of the carving process and how it is inherently linked to meaning. I eventually used this theme in my work.

After college it was a matter of working out how to make a living with the minimum of compromise – not easy. However I had a skill to sell and it was a matter of finding out where I could sell it.

Primary Project

My first project was a sculpture playground for a school in Norfolk. The Sandringham Estate forestry department were wonderful. They supplied all the tree-trunks, took away all the turf, and delivered several tonnes of bark chips – which were the only thing the school had to pay for.

I worked solidly throughout the month, carving mainly with the chainsaw, and just adding the details with chisels. The children were able to watch the day-to-day progress of their playground, from big tractors arriving with timber to the finished whale, dolphin, shells, boat, balancing snake and jumping toadstools.

I learned a great deal from this opportunity; organising materials, having to work to a deadline, and fulfilling expectations. Everyone was very pleased with the result, and once I had documented the work I was able to use the slides to apply for other work that I saw advertised in *Artists' Newsletter*.

Dersingham First School Sculpture Playground. Left to Right: shell seat, dolphins, snake, toadstools, spiral shell, boat. Whale and stepping logs in foreground

Playing with fire

No other work came my way for a year, and in the meantime I became a member of the 'Starlings Art Group'. This resulted in a group show at Tennant's Auctioneers in Leyburn North Yorkshire. The work I produced for this show continued on from college preoccupations, but was beginning to become more organic. I had also started playing with fire, both for the beautiful blackness which this affect achieved and the depth it gave the cavities and hollows. I enjoyed introducing an element of risk into the process. The carving was carried out initially with the chainsaw, then a Bosch angle-grinder with an Arbortech woodcarver disc. Later that year, I re-worked *Hollow* for an exhibition at the Kings Lyn Arts Centre, removing more of the inside and putting a hand-carved surface onto the outside.

Handcarving has become a more important part of the process in my more recent work – time is the eternal enemy, but I try to find an equilibrium between using powertools as far as

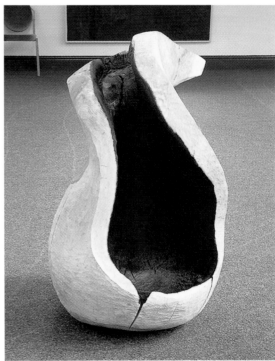

Hollow Growth, 1993

Work in progress on
Hollow, December 1992

possible into the process, and then moving on to the chisel and getting down to the nitty-gritty. It's when the hand-carving starts that the real decision making begins.

I have collected twenty-six chisels over the years. Many are second-hand but I generally buy Henry Taylors for the specialised shapes and the larger chisels. They range from 38mm, 1½in No.10 and No.5 down to 2mm, 1⁄16in No.11 and a 3mm, 1⁄8in No.5. I have a few spoon-bent gouges and have recently found a beautiful Mathieson 5mm, 3⁄16 forebent 90° v-tool. I've come to the conclusion that you can't have too many chisels and I continue to collect whenever I have some spare cash!

First figure

In March this year I was approached by a landscape architect, given my name by Chris Sell, another woodcarver in the area. This commission was to carve a 'guardian' and some simple log seats for a nature garden being developed at Walkergate Junior School, Newcastle. The project took two weeks to carry out. Initially I spent an afternoon with a class of children thinking about designs and doing lots of drawings with them. I like to involve the children in the process as much as possible, and whilst I was carving, groups regularly came out to visit me, ask questions and see how the project was progressing.

The main piece took the form of a life-size figure emerging from a beautiful elm trunk. I had planned the figure to have a leaf-shaped mask, but as the carving developed the children made it clear to me that a proper face was needed. Although I'd never carved a human face before and I had already roughed out the mask, I went ahead and thoroughly enjoyed the challenge.

It was quite thrilling to attempt to make the wood come 'alive'. I used the saw to rough-out the figure, and then went to work with the chisels, occasionally returning to the saw when I decided to remove a large area: either cutting a chunk off, taking curved slices away, gradually tightening a curve, or using the base of the saw nose to nibble away at smaller areas by running over the surface.

The rest of the figure has a long flowing gown, most of the lower part is obscured by a large leaf-shaped shield which conveniently covers the right hand. I had to carve the left hand however, which gripped a long sword. It was a matter of simplifying the form as far as possible to keep within time, concentrating on the difficult areas and maximising the impact.

Left *Guardian*. Commission for the nature garden at Walkergate Junior School

Top from left to right
● Earth, a highback seat showing tree with roots exposed
● Fire is represented by the sun
● Water shows clouds with rain falling into the waves
● Air with hair angled up and back, giving depth to the piece

Right **The face of the air seat**

Positioning the piece

When the piece was finished I set about preparing the foundations. An 18–20in, 460–510mm deep pit was dug, approximately the same diameter as the base and ¾in, 20mm reinforcing bars were put into the base and sides of the pit, protruding about 6in, 150mm. Heavy duty plastic was pinned to the base of the sculpture to minimize any contact between concrete and timber, and ½in, 13mm bars were sharpened and hammered into the base. The pit was then filled with concrete, the piece lifted up, and eased into position making sure the cement oozed around the reinforcing bars. The figure was then propped so that it sat straight and did not move whilst the cement set. I was very pleased with the result, and it was certainly a

'I like to involve the children in the process as much as possible'

confidence boost to know that I could carve a reasonably convincing human figure!

Furniture in the forest

In June last year, a project I had begun to set up the summer before, finally came to fruition. I had approached the Forestry Commission at Kielder with the idea of carrying out some work for them (itching to return to the forest and do some work, albeit in a different capacity). Chris Probert, the Recreation Officer, was willing to fund the materials and practicalities, but it was up to me to raise the money to cover my fee and expenses. To cut a very long story short, I brought in an organisation called Arts Resource to take over the management of the project and fund-raise the deficit from Northern Arts. Chris wanted functional work, seating and a table, and it was up to me to make them as sculptural as possible.

I produced designs based on the four elements, earth, air, water and the sun – four high-backed seats each featuring one of the elements, around a simple rough-hewn table, and a bench which incorporated a relief carving of the elements acting on a tree. The designs were accepted and I went off at the beginning of June to a sawmill and picked three large elm trunks.

With the timber on site the first task was to allocate all the pieces, and begin the 'primary breakdown', to use some sawmill jargon. I initially cut two 5ft, 1.5m lengths from the trunks, which were to be sliced in half to form the four chairbacks. Next I chose the widest log for the bench-end which had to fit the biggest carving. This entailed rip-cutting with the saw which was very hard work. It is possible to buy a special rip-chain but I have not experimented with one yet, instead I reduced the angle of the cutting teeth to approximately 15° which seemed to work quite well.

I have a Husqvarna 266 XP chainsaw which is ideally suited to cutting softwoods – high revving rather than high torque – but I tune it down slightly and so long as I keep it sharp (I retouch the teeth after about 10ft, 3m of rip-cutting), it seems to do the job very well. The logs were on average about 30in, 760mm diameter, so with the 20in, 510mm bar I had to cut one side, stopping regularly to make sure the cut was straight, then turn the trunk right over and run through the other side. The most efficient cutting position was to cut with the top of the bar, and with the nose slightly ahead of the engine: this meant I was using a 'pulling chain' and so long as the chain was sharp, it pulled it's way through the timber and I just had to keep the saw straight.

The 'sun' carving was the piece I started with. Initially I kept the log on it's side and shaved off much of the sapwood with the saw, keeping the maximum depth of the log at the

Earth, air, fire (the sun), water,1994.
View of the four chairs, table and bench at Kielder Castle

'The public reaction was
tremendous... it was great
to have so much
enthusiastic feedback'

base. Then I turned the piece face upwards and propped it at a 30° angle. This enabled me to continue roughing out in a reasonably comfortable position. Once a reasonable convex 'face' was achieved, I began carving the hemisphere with chisels and pushing back the background. When satisfied with the evenness of the face, I drew the features in with chalk and marked a central line from chin to forehead, so that the face leaned slightly to the left and prevented the piece being too symmetrical. The flames were added later, drawn on so that they wrapped around the chair.

'Air' came next and had to be composed on a vertical plane. I decided to position the face quite low and as far forward as possible. The hair was then angled up and back, creating a degree of depth and ensuring that the carving was bottom heavy. This allowed me to lift it upright to view it periodically without assistance. The face took several days to carve. I kept leaving it for intervals, to decide what I thought was wrong with it before continuing.

'Earth' was problematic at the design stage because I wasn't sure what image to choose. Using the tree seemed appropriate for the Forestry Commission, and to signify 'earth' the roots were carved. I used the saw to carve the crown of the tree, and randomly carved snaking roots spread out over the lower section.

When carving 'water', I used a similar saw technique for the cloud. The large water droplets were drawn on and the background taken back about 3in, 75mm with the saw. They were then carved into nice bottom-heavy drops and the background was given a carved surface. I tried to get as much movement as I could with the pattern at the bottom and wrapped the waves around the surface to heighten the three-dimensional feel.

The composite carving for the bench was the last to be carried out, and is more of a relief-carving than the others. The main problem was to simplify the design to enable me to fit all of the elements into the composition; I therefore dispensed with rain-drops and sun-rays, and used the wind-blown tree and wind as the main focus.

All the staff were very cooperative, especially towards the end when they were digging foundations, doing all the cementing and clearing up after me! They were also very interested in the work itself, and enjoyed being able to see the pieces take shape.

The public reaction was also tremendous. It meant lots of interruptions but it was great to have so much enthusiastic feedback. The visitors were a complete cross-section of the public and for the most part I found this very interesting and stimulating. They certainly appreciated being able to watch an artist at work, ask questions and discuss the work progress with me. Many looked forward to returning when the project was completed. The only real problems were caused by the weather, but this only reinforced the appropriateness of the subject matter.

I thoroughly enjoyed the residency, and got a lot out of the experience both personally and in developing my work. I was able to fully concentrate on the sculptures for the whole month, making maximum use of the daylight hours before retiring to my tent and settling down for the night. ●

Since completing a Fine Art degree in 1992, Richard Caink has built up a portfolio of projects including play sculptures for schools and sculptures for public places. Essentially self-taught, his experience has enabled him to improve his carving skills. He intends to complete a sculpture MA in the near future, which will enable him to concentrate more on the 'fine art' side of his work and do some part-time teaching to supplement his income.
Richard is a member of the Starlings Group, and is represented by the Streltsy Fine Artists' Agency.

FLIGHTS OF FANCY

Judith Nicoll discovers how Jonathan Fearnhead creates his mythological figures

Some people have what it takes. However little we know about a subject, we recognise excellence when we see it. When I am lucky enough to meet such a carver, I want to know not only how he uses his skills, but what other processes are involved in the planning and execution. Then I want to find out about the individual and why he is outstanding.

Despite coming from a family of scientists, Jonathan Fearnhead, now aged 27, decided at school he was to spend his life working with wood. He started carving when he was about 13, but jokes he was cutting the garden down with a saw when he was only three.

He learned his first steps in three dimensions while working on balsa aeroplanes. He insisted they had to fly or they were no good. This was perhaps an early indication of his lack of interest in abstract carving. His aeroplanes were flown to destruction and then new ones made with faults corrected and the design improved.

As a child he was free to experiment and do what he wanted. Tellingly there was no television. The house was surrounded by trees and he grew up playing with wood. He and his brother directed their imagination into playing war games, and Jonathan was inspired by *Lord of the Rings*, myths and legends.

Early influences

Some of his ideas are gleaned from a fantasy world "which is a good place for a beginner to start without leaving himself open to criticism," he tells me.

When asked about his early influences and role models, Jonathan admits he was fascinated by the

sculptures of Leonardo, Rodin and Michelangelo. He liked their "soft, fluid lines which are absolutely perfect, their mapping of the surface that has no depth stop. These sorts of forms can't be measured but come from understanding," he says. His more contemporary role models are well-known carvers such as Ian Norbury and Ray Gonzalez.

After school, different jobs provided Jonathan with useful experience and training. After working in a local precision engineering factory, he was head-hunted by an architectural joiner. With this company, he restored an 18th century staircase in a famous London hotel.

After removing 350 years of paint, new pieces had to be scarfed on, new capitals made and repetitive details such as working on acanthus leaves on a dado rail.

Competitive challenge

During this time he had been carving for himself and entering junior competitions. In the first year he entered he won a gold award for a knight in armour which was based on a picture in a school history book.

It was about 6in, 15cm high and mounted on ebony. "The surface was flowing and it had a bit of life" says Jonathan. Maurice Lund won that year and kindly gave Jonathan £20 to buy some tools.

Other chisels came as Christmas presents or from pocket-money saved up. Ashley Iles have also helped a great deal. They grind his chisels especially thin, which is how he likes them. In retrospect he believes learning to carve with few tools taught him to make full use of each tool.

He can't remember how many gold medals he has won now, but he admits he aims to win. He finds competitions are an incentive and a challenge but he has never aimed a piece at a competition.

Above **A young Jonathan Fearnhead working on a dragon carving**

Left *Gandalf* (1984)

The Wayward Wizard

If he is happy with a finished piece, then he enters it. In all his carving he aims for "the highest standard of craftsmanship and finish since it is these aspects that count most heavily in the eyes of the judges. That someone will be looking for flaws, and knows where to look, is a great spur to do your best," he comments.

I asked him which winning pieces were special to him and instantly he replied *Bottom* and *Samurai with Sword*. He enjoys seeing his old carvings and remembering certain details. Even so, he regards each carving as a practice or maquette for the next one.

It is important to be critical of your work and this is where competition is also valuable. There are standards of craftsmanship to achieve, but the design and whether it works or not are open to judgement. He believes going to shows has been an integral part of his learning, as is teaching others.

Teaching benefits

When we were discussing his teaching, a number of pointers to his carving approach appeared. Jonathan started as a steward at the national shows when he was 14 years old. He was asked to demonstrate aged 18, when Maurice Lund was unwell. Then he was invited by Peter Benson from Essex to join his evening classes as an unpaid assistant.

It is quite obvious Jonathan loves teaching. He admits to learning a lot by being confronted with so many different types of carvings, each with its own problems. He notices many adults are frightened of getting things wrong and he recognises starting young is an advantage, because whatever you do is considered good.

In a few pupils he recognises his own uninhibited attack on the wood. He likes to rip into his wood to rough it out and if it goes wrong, he throws it away. It only takes two days to re-rough it and few go wrong. Those which get shelved are normally ones in which he has lost interest.

He admits he's not the best planner. He does little drawing and researches on the hoof. As he talks about two of his projects, I can see the thinking and working out which is happening as the carving takes shape.

But I get the impression he persuades his pupils to get a project completely together before setting forth. He tries to remember what it

Left *Centaur* (1985)

Above **All Jonathan's carvings start as simple line drawings to get the right balance and movement. He says the lines of the sculpture are the most important part and no amount of fine detailing can disguise poor design**

A carving is won or lost in the first few days of getting movement, balance and proportion

was like when he first started, and knows they might not have enough skills to complete an idea without breakage or injury.

He helps them to re-design without losing the essence of their idea. He likes them to have complete freedom to choose their subject and helps them 'pin down' part of the carving as early as possible.

He explains, for example, the positioning of the head in the right place when carving a figure. It is then possible to work out the various positions of all the other parts of the body.

"This can be done so you can get close to the desired shape, and at the same time leave wood in the right places for later detail and design adjustments."

A carving is won or lost in the first few days of getting movement, balance and proportion. The muscles and finer structures of the detail bring these out, but only later. Structure comes first, and then the detail is the icing on the cake.

He helps pupils see how curves change shape from different angles. He is famous for asking students to knock the corners off, as he does not like squareness. He wants them to appreciate what he calls quality of line by looking from all angles at their piece and seeing where each line goes and flows, for when each line is right then the surfaces will also be right.

He remembers being told to draw round, like a Michelin man, to get volume. He teaches people to work on the outside first before diving in. It is the nature of a beginner to work on a convex surface, and he wants them to achieve the main outside shape before starting on the hollows, and then committing themselves to the under-cutting. They need to turn the piece at all angles and look, because they need to see all angles to judge depth.

Design is the most difficult aspect of carving to teach, not the manual skills. We agreed most things can be taught, but when someone comes with a knack or special ability it does make a difference. He points out the superb sculptors of the past were usually superb draughtsmen.

Smooth surface

Manual sculpting is important to Jonathan, he likes a chiselled finish, and a finer one than he says he has yet achieved. It should look smooth and rounded, but not with millions of facets. "There is something appealing in a shape made up entirely with chisel cuts," he tells me. "If one cut stands out, then it's wrong, and if it is in the wrong direction then it is interrupting the flow."

He refers back to the smoothness of Michelangelo's work. He feels his own are still too rough. He tells his pupils to find a chisel near enough the contour they want so they don't facet the surface too much.

In Grinling Gibbons' work, it is possible to see the chisel marks, but it's smooth. Although it looks like three cuts, it is thousands. The trick is to use these marks to emphasise the design. He wishes to have enough tools to cover all shapes, but 3,000 gouges are out of the question! He admits to using between ten and twenty most of the time, out of his collection of several hundred.

His favourite tool is a gouge with a fine metal section. So many modern tools have too much metal on them. He shows me a shallow gouge and demonstrates how he can effortlessley slide it in to a depth of ½in, 13mm as the resistance is so low.

It helps to maintain a shallow gouge angle for cutting, and moreover allows the reverse to be used so he can also cut on a convex angle. Most gouges can only be used on one side or they just dig in. He loves its flexibility, mobility and manoeuvrability. He also has special tools for hooking out in the hollows, rather than pushing a gouge in to cut, and he designs his own tools.

Lamination

Jonathan and I discussed three small issues which often loom large in the carving world. I asked if those who carve from just one piece should be revered. Jonathan cheerfully told me which pieces were added to his carving and why, but he challenges people to identify them.

Samurai Warrior

Whether you have to add pieces is determined at the design stage. With complicated carving some areas will be strong, but others will be the weak short grain. There is a special skill in adding pieces so the blend is acceptable.

Anticipating the grain and colour is difficult, particularly bearing in mind the reflections in the light. In his carving of the Samurai warrior, he sandwiched a long grain piece of wood between two end-grain veneers to create the impression of a bevelled sword blade. They were laminated and looked appropriate because of the different shades and the reflection of light.

"It isn't enough to drill a hole and whack in a piece of dowel! The hand has to appear to be gripping the shaft, and careful attention must be paid to the shape of the sword handle, as it will affect the way the hand is carved."

Crack attack

A common concern for many carvers are cracks in the wood, but they do not bother Jonathan, he sorts them out when he's finished. If he needs to remedy a crack, he chooses wood of a following grain and similar colour and cuts a piece to fit. We agreed wood is a living material and novices should not worry about cracks since they can be remedied.

The third issue I often hear debated is how a carving should be sealed and finished. Jonathan has recently taken to sealing his wood with several coats of thinned out cellulose or melamine lacquer which penetrates the wood deeply.

When it starts to lie on the surface, he lets it dry. Then he mixes wax and cellulose thinners with a splash of linseed oil and brushes this into the wood with a fairly stiff brush. The thinners in the wax dissolve the excess surface lacquer. The oil is added to stop the brush, or later the cloth, from sticking to the wood.

This process leaves a clean finish which won't clog the fine detail. He emphasises extreme care when heating the wax and the oil. He uses a double saucepan and turns off the heat before adding thinners. He applies it only in a well-ventilated room.

Terrifying troll

Then we looked at his current work, a personal indulgence as he calls it. It is a troll and called *A Good Day's Hunting*. It is designed to be viewed from all sides. There are not abstract or graceful forms here but clever balanced design and storytelling.

There is a lot happening and the viewer becomes involved with the sculpture. The troll has dreadful incisors and a miscreant's gleeful, yet half-apologetic face surrounded by human heads. He hides a child's head behind his back.

His idea started from a tinted picture in the *National Geographic Magazine* of a human hunter with buffalo, and he changed the subject. It is the largest of his carvings so far, standing just under 3ft, 0.9m, with a 15 x 15in, 380 x 380mm width and depth.

The elbows and knees are close to the original edges of the piece of lime. As always, he left plenty of wood in the base to allow for changes, which he needed as he found the knee dropped and he was able to extend the leg.

When roughing out, he knew the side profile he wanted with the stomach and bottom stuck out, and so he could see how far the head had to go back. Once he had decided on the face angle he was then able to go in and remove the unwanted wood around the head. He is now reaching the 'buzz' time when he can start mapping the detail. Maybe we will see it in a national competition. ●

Top **Detail of the troll's head from *A Good Day's Hunting***
Right **Jonathan Fearnhead working on his latest carving, *A Good Day's Hunting***

The front of Uri Panov's home is a gallery of his work

SIBERIAN EXILE

LES LEE

A trip to Siberia uncovers the fantastic work of Uri Panor.

'I'm sure he lives somewhere around here,' said Lena. She was the courier-interpreter that One-Europe Travel had engaged to shepherd me around Irkutsk, and the neighbouring area of Siberia. Urik, where I was staying, is a little village strung along the sides of the road leading north up into the Arctic.

I'd really come to see lake Baikal, the world's deepest lake. It is reputed to hold more than a fifth of the planet's freshwater supplies and has a wonderful selection of flora and fauna; including fish and seals found nowhere else.

After more than 8,000 bum-numbing kilometres on the Trans Siberian Railway, I was glad to get off for a couple of days. Then I discovered that there was a carver living nearby. The Siberian forests cover about six

A figure from the Spanish Inquisition wields both dagger and sword

million square miles. Silver birches are probably the most common trees, but other types of birch abound, together with larches, pines, aspen and maple. The rivers and streams bear willows and poplars along their banks. Timber is a major resource.

Searching Siberia

The village we were seeking lies about two thirds of the way from Irkutsk to Listvyanka beside the lake. It's called Bolshaya Rechka, which translates as big river village, and lies beside the powerful Angara river, which flows from the lake. Local legend has it that there are 333 other rivers, but they all flow into the lake.

It was cold, but all the snow had gone and the bright spring sun threw thin spears of light through the gloomy trees and across the bonnet of the car. We splashed along the muddy road, asking directions when we met a rare pedestrian. After back-tracking and two changes of course we emerged from the woods, and suddenly we were there.

Beside the road overlooking the wide river, on a strip of grass liberally covered with wood chips, was a white haired and bearded woodcarver; looking like a blue-eyed forest goblin wearing a heavy blue lumberjack shirt and the traditional Russian high boots. Busily carving one of the trees which stood outside his small front garden, he sat surrounded by a gallery of political, allegorical and phantasmagorical portrait heads, fashioned from the gnarled burrs and truncated branches of other trees.

'He sat surrounded by a gallery of political allegorical and phantasmagorical portrait heads'

Heavily bearded revolutionary gargoyles jostle with ascetic biblical saints. Political heavies such as Kaganovich and the evil Beria whisper into Stalin's ear. A hooded figure, depicting the Spanish Inquisition, brandishes a dagger and a cross. A hand grips a Mauser pistol. A small

panel proclaims Liberté, Egalité, Fraternité. Lower down on the bole of the tree a flag bears a Cyrillic slogan I could not recognise.

The motif was continued on to nearby objects. The top of a fencepost bore a shaggy head, heavily bearded and moustachioed. The gates into the yard were surmounted by a pair of wriggly serpents to discourage intruders.

The carver of this wonderland is Uri Andreyevitch Panov. A sprightly 71 years old, he has taken more than ten years to sculpt this unqiue frontage to his home. Born in Kharkov in the Ukraine, he served in the Soviet Army during the war, before being imprisoned for political offences from 1941 to 1951. In 1956 he came to his present home at Bolshaya Rechka in the Siberian woodlands.

Originally an artist and painter he is a self-taught woodcarver. His versatility and execution are remarkable. Each portrait head exhibits a different expression or emotion, and all are encompassed and enhanced by the flowing forms and

Uri Andreyevitch Panov at work

Stalin at the top of the tree; Kaganovich whispers in his ear and a satyr grins below them

The side of the
house is adorned
with carvings and
the skull of an elk

undulations of the wood. All the trees he has carved are pines. Each one is carefully protected to withstand the rigours of the harsh Siberian winters.

House and exhibition

His house is basically a large log cabin. It is decorated with a fretted fascia below a heavy moulding, which runs under the lower edge of the corrugated roof. There are no gutters; a similarly decorated board adorns the eaves. The window frames are surrounded by a wide façade, adorned with mouldings, and on the top a large headboard carries more fretwork surmounted by carved scrolls, and supported by small carved brackets. Two panels on the front elevation bear what appear to be abstract assemblages of intertwined natural forms of wood.

Writhing snakes protect the gates to the yard

Uri Panov carving one of the trees in front of his house, many of his carvings are from early Soviet history

Another view of Uri's current project reveals a woman in a Phrygian cap and French Revolutionary slogan. There is also a portrait of Lenin at the base of the tree

All the decorative woodwork is finished in white and yellow paint, the structural logs are untreated except for a possible covering of a natural coloured preservative. On the side in the yard another panel bears high relief carved double busts of a male and female, beside the skull and antlers of an elk. Below, another collection of relief heads includes one suspiciously like of Beatle, George Harrison.

I could have stayed all day just watching Uri Panov work, but Georgi, the car driver, was drumming his fingers on the steering wheel, and Lena came to drag me away, protesting. She had to remind me, I'd forgotten all about our trip to lake Baikal. ■

CONSIDERING CARVING

ED SAYLAN

Californian woodcarver Anton Fuetsch discusses his approach to carving.

When talking about woodcarving a common assumption is that a naturalistic approach is good, but in wood it doesn't work. There is one reason for this, the material itself. Wood requires more difficult work techniques than denser materials do, therefore it has to be stylised. This alone leads away from a naturalistic approach. This is an area where many misconceptions come about.

If you do realistic, naturalistic, representational work, which is mostly traditional, you have to find a way to cut the wood in a logical way. In other areas of sculpture, not just for wood there are other limitations to realism. You have to stand far enough away from a piece to be able to see the complete contours. When you step close enough to actually hold the tool on the work you cannot see all of the contour.

There is another problem concerned with distance from the work, as an example take the carving of a life-size figure. In order to take in the complete figure, without distortions of perspective, you must be a certain distance away, but this may be too far away to get details you may want. These are contradictions that force us to move away from realism.

There should be a balance between the contour and the necessary amount of detail, one should not outweigh the other. The early Greeks had that harmony, when you look at it stays with you. A certain amount of detail gives you the feeling of being close, being intimate. Having a contour gives you the message of being itself. When someone walks towards you on the street you get a feeling about them from their posture. When you get closer that's lost. If you have that balance I think the combination works.

Historical lessons

If you look carefully at woodcarving from the past you may be surprised at just how

Anton at work on old clock case needing some repair

stylised some of the old 'naturalistic' work is; especially from the baroque period to the nineteenth century. When woodcarving was at its height, carvers stylised. They did not exaggerate, but they accentuated certain details and left others out. They kept certain flows and ornaments having to do with the pattern of the wood grain, and the way the work was to be displayed in the church, castle or mansion. The proportions of these buildings were generally bigger than most houses, and the work far away, therefore the carving had to be more dramatic because of the distance from the viewers.

In order to be effective the modern carver should be exposed to that early work. If they are not they have to discover its techniques on their own. Most sculptors can do this, but its a long and difficult road; repeating the mistakes of trial and error. The techniques the old carvers were using are just as valid today as they were in the past because they have to do with distance, light, and material — things that haven't changed, and that can be applied to any subject. Subjects or themes change but these underlying things don't. In order to have an effective piece you must know these techniques, then the piece will be lively. The things that have changed over the years are the themes.

'Knowing a shape helps you to cut it.'

We seem to be closer to nature today, people seem to feel passionately about nature, the seasons, anything that grows; despite or perhaps because most people live so far from them. We realise the vulnerability of these things today, more so than 200 years ago, when people didn't have the same sense of fragility. They took nature for granted. What people want now, even though it's decorative, usually relates to nature. We now feel more affinity with the material because we are experiencing something we never did before, the fragility and vulnerability of nature. Our pre-decessors would not have believed that nature was so frail, we have the evidence of this. It is an idea that didn't enter people's minds until maybe 50 years ago.

Historical development

Today it's still true that some commissions come from churches; such as I did recently. In the old days the church was part of the state — rich and influential — and wood-carving, like other trades and crafts was

A wall piece of Antons showing the effects of two very different lighting approaches

heavily dependant on such institutions. Technology didn't exist to the extent it does today, so craftsmanship was pushed to a point where craftsmen could work with great precision. To hand make clocks and machinery required a minimum degree of precision, if it was not attained the machine would not work. This level of craftsmanship was reflected in other areas as well.

Production methods were developed, and at some time in the nineteenth century bulk production was introduced. Carvings were produced by the thousands. Machinery became more sophisticated, but in order to sell to the huge market things were modified to make production faster. Products were modified more and more, until they became unappealing.

The craftsman was not appreciated until hand work and custom building was rediscovered around 1900. The guilds were revived and it seemed that a new era was about to begin. Art Nouveau, the Arts and Crafts movement, and Art Deco all came along and used carving; not only because of tradition but for the appeal of the wood itself.

In my work my customers are asking for carvings that reflect much of what I've been discussing; and affinity for hand work, fine craftsmanship. They like and appreciate things made by hand.

Woodcarving is addictive — for the carver that is. The ability to make something of beauty has to be repeated, as in music. One can take a piece of wood and, with a workbench and a few sharp tools, make something that someone will buy and appreciate. The fact that I can support myself doing this completes a circle that is very appealing to me. I have to deal with people, and the exchange of money for work shows respect, and is a statement about the work.

Colouring wood

I don't do any painting on carvings unless it's required; it seems to me that the grain and material should be shown. If you're going to paint it other materials could be utilised, rather than wood, to achieve the same thing. Whatever the reason, the finish of a piece should be planned from the beginning, the finish should not be applied as an afterthought, especially if it is to be coloured.

Showing the material isn't just about the colour and grain of the wood, it's using the way the wood flows; the style of carving can add to the feeling of the wood without texturing or colouring. I think that this is where wood character starts, when you find what is already there. This is something that contemporary woodworkers have very much in mind today.

A maquette and sketch of a fireplace surround. Anton uses these to show his client the details

Commercialism

The danger in the commercial approach is that people associate fine detail with fine art, and in order to sell quickly detail is added to the surface. This makes it easy to distinguish between commercial and folk carving. When we talk about the areas that are not genuine, such as commercial carving, adding colour just to sell moves away from the real thing. In the fourteenth and fifteenth centuries colour was added for different reasons. Obviously it was not done for commercial reasons, as the carvers couldn't reproduce works in great numbers. These carvers coloured their work to symbolise things, so aspects of them were easy to identify. Gilding has its own effect, but also shows prestige.

The work in progress, with a small carved figure that was used as a model

On the commercial side, we now see items from the Philippines, Bali, Mexico, and elsewhere round the world, and you can see the loss of traditional values. They are very good with detail, but not necessarily good with contour.

Carving subjects

Wherever I go, whatever I do, whatever I look at, I always try to think about how I would carve it. How would I move the tool? How the grain will react when I move the tool through it is a major concern; you have to be able to resolve it in the material. If you design something that you can't carve then you may force the tools, and the work will not be good; it will feel awkward. You might chip the wood, have the tool at the wrong angle, and not get the sheen that it's supposed to have.

Knowing a shape helps you to cut it. If you're certain of the shape you can move the tool. If you're not certain about the shape, and you have to search for it, you will probably remove too much; it will appear flat or stiff, and the hollows in the work will be too much. If you're not certain you remove a little here and a little there, and pretty soon too much is gone, and you'll have that awkward feeling. Whether your work is abstract or representational it's the

Details of the fire surround showing how stylisation gives a naturalistic appearance

Carving considerations

same; the relationship between mass and space.

My first consideration in carving a piece is the site it will occupy. Where does it sit? Is it to be mounted on a wall? Will it be free standing? Where is the light coming from? Where will the viewer be? If it's to be above eye level you must consider proportions. How will it remind viewers of the tree itself? How many elongated shapes can I have in there to follow the flow of the tree. How many spaces should I have and how shall I balance the hollow space with the mass? How many long lines will go to the bottom? How will I make the contours reflect the images I want? How much small detail will I put inside the piece?

To help resolve these questions I sketch a clay model, roughly one-third or half size; no fine details unless the client wants to be reassured about them. For a life-size piece one should have a model. If the subject is completely new to you then a model is required, if it is small than a sketch will do. Wood selection is sometimes up to the client. If someone wants something in a really dense wood it might very well change the shape of the piece. Long flowing lines don't lend themselves to dark dense wood; they're more stone like and the piece might become more circular. Something for a table top might require that circular composition — something below eye level. These are the first decisions that have to be made by artist/carvers — to be articulated by them in wood. ■

Fire surround, ready for delivery. Finishing will be done in the home

MOTHER FIGURES

Jackie McNamee explains how she explores maternity and images of women in her sculptures

While I was at college I had the opportunity to work in a number of different media, including stone, clay, cast bronze and metal. But I chose wood for the images I wanted to make because it was the most enjoyable material with which to work.

The inspiration for my sculptures comes from various sources – old Irish stone figures, early bird-goddess culture, and also how things like motherhood, war, media representations and domestic expectations affect us.

As well as carving I also make woodcut prints on the same themes as my sculpture, using a set of Chinese woodcut tools and sheets of medium density fibreboard. I print these on the relief press at the Edinburgh Printmakers' Workshop. I find they enhance the sculptures when I am exhibiting and, because of their size, are easy to sell.

It is never a problem getting wood for small pieces. I have used cherry (*Prunus avium*) many times, although anything over 6in, 150mm diameter tends to split badly unless the log is first cut lengthways. I used this method for *Bernie the Bolt and Donna the Dart*, which is about women in TV gameshows, with particular reference to Bob Monkhouse. I used beech (*Fagus sylvatica*) branches for the babies in *Did She Have One Baby or Two Babies?*

For larger pieces I go to the district council's parks' department sawmill in Edinburgh, where I can get trees which have

Top left **Maternity Clinic (1992) a woodcut print**
Top right **Starting work on a new piece at the Edinburgh Sculpture Workshop**

Above left **Bernie The Bolt And Donna the Dart** (1993)
Above right **Did She Have One Baby Or Two Babies?** (1992)

been felled because of old age or disease. There is a lot of elm (*Ulmus hollandica*) at the moment because of Dutch elm disease.

Electric start

I begin by doing a number of drawings to get my ideas on paper, and then I make a small maquette in clay, so I have a three-dimensional image from which to work. Having a chainsaw makes getting a piece of work under way quick and easy. I use a Stihl E-20 electric chainsaw as I am generally working inside the workshop or near a power source.

I prefer an electric saw to a petrol one because it does not create exhaust fumes and it is easier to start. The E-20 has a powerful enough motor to cut through the biggest trunk I could want to tackle. Although I have been using chainsaws for a number of years I am aware of their potential danger, and always wear protective leggings and headgear.

Most of my carving tools come from Henry Taylor, although I was given a set of extremely old small tools for fine details in my final year at college, which are wonderful. I use a nylon mallet, and I usually go through two of my large gouge handles for each big sculpture I work on.

Big birds

For a large piece I do a lot of roughing out with the saw. *Dehiscence* (a botanical term for a pod splitting in two to release the seed) is made from two pieces of lime (*Tilia vulgaris*), which is a delightful wood to carve. I cut slices into the trunk I used for the mother bird, and then knocked them off with an adze or with my 2in, 50mm Henry Taylor allongee tool (no.3798), which is invaluable for the first stage of any carving.

After getting the shape well established, I cut the piece in two and hollowed out both the body and the head sections using the chainsaw. I finished off with an Arbortech attachment on an angle grinder, so the baby bird would fit inside the body of the mother, like a Russian doll.

Above left *Dehiscence* **(1992)**
Above right *Matriline* **(1992)**

Colour emphasises the form, makes the work more interesting, and has an historic precedent

I also use the chainsaw on smaller pieces, as for the zigzags and the hollowing of the alcove for *Matriline*, which is made from one piece of sycamore sliced lengthways, and for the elm sunburst of *Confinement*, which I then carved to fit the curves on top of a block of Kilkenny limestone. The figure inside is cherry and stands on a platform of elm.

Open house

As well as providing whole tree trunks, the council sawmill slices trees into planks of various sizes and thicknesses to order. I used slices of elm to make *Mère Ouvrante*.

The idea for this piece came from pictures I had seen of Vierge Ouvrantes, which are figures of the Virgin Mary which open up to reveal scenes from the life of Jesus. I wanted this to have a domestic theme and say something about women's home lives.

I made the cupboard from three planks of elm, which were 6ft x 24 x 1½in, 1.8m x 610 x 38mm. They were freshly cut and smelled strong for several months as they gradually dried. The front was made from two widths of elm, and the doors were cut out with a jigsaw and held in place with brass hinges.

I joined the front to the sides, which were made from six pieces of plank dovetail-jointed together, with a lot of countersunk screws to prevent warping, and then I fitted small pieces of dowel to hide the screw heads. The sycamore (*Acer pseudoplatanus*) legs slot into round holes in the base of the cupboard, and the head and neck (cherry) slot into the top.

The baby bird was also made from cherry, and the spoons and forks were cut from elm plank with a bandsaw and finished by hand. These were then attached to thin strips of metal which I riveted to the back of the cupboard, so when the side doors are unlatched and opened, the spoons and forks vibrate and rattle against each other. I carved the flowers on the outside in relief using a U-shaped curved tool.

I also used a slice of wood to make the box for the figures in *Did She Have One Baby Or Two Babies*? The idea for this piece came from a remark I overheard someone making about his friend. He knew she had children but just couldn't remember how many.

I was given a large oak (*Quercus spp*) plank which had been discarded because it had warped and split slightly. It was beautiful wood to work with, and one day I would love to get hold of a whole oak, but since I only use trees which have had to be cut down I may have to wait a long time.

Figure painting

Once I have finished a piece I rub it down with medium grade sandpaper and then paint it using Craig and Rose emulsion paints. Craig and Rose have a wonderful selection of strong colours, and I use the paint well watered down so it sinks into the wood and the grain still shows through.

Some purist woodcarvers have told me they find this sacrilegious and an insult to the beauty of the wood, but I find the colour emphasises the form, makes the work more interesting, and also has an historic precedent in religious and folk art.

I leave parts of the carving unpainted and rub back the painted areas a little with sandpaper before sealing it with a layer of matt varnish and then applying Anderson Gibb and Wilson prepared white wax polish.

Tall order

I really enjoy working on large pieces, and I am fortunate to have room to do this at the Edinburgh Sculpture Workshop, and also during the summer at Ardess Craft Centre.

Last year I was given a 7 x 3ft, 2.1 x 0.9m beech trunk. This old tree had been growing on a ridge above the craft centre but had to be cut down as it was rotten in the middle. I used this to make the first of my large female figures, which I called *Woman in Black*.

She wore a full length bell-shaped black dress, and was holding two empty picture frames.

Woman in Black was based on what I heard of groups of women in the former Yugoslavia, and in other countries where they have lost family and friends in conflicts, and who wear black and meet in public places in peaceful protest against war.

Top left **Confinement**
Above **Mère Ouvrante (1992)**
Far left **Woman in Black**
(1993)
Left **That Year**

I usually go
through two of
my large gouge
handles for each
big sculpture

The next figure I made was 7ft, 2.1m tall, in sycamore with an elm base, and I called it *That Year*. The figure and three birds were carved from one piece and the weak points where the birds met the figure presented some problems.

Rather than have a plain expanse of black skirt, I carved a relief pattern of feathers which echoed the birds' wings. To give this tall, heavy figure stability I got a large chunk of elm. In the centre I fitted a rectangular piece of ½in, 13mm thick metal plate with a perpendicular 6in, 150mm length of 1in, 25mm bar welded to the centre.

I then drilled up the centre of the figure's base, and removed a rectangle of wood around it with a chisel so when the figure slid on to the bar, the metal plate locked it in position. I was pleased with this carving, which won a prize at the Royal Scottish Academy, and is now housed in a beautiful wood and glass room in Fife.

In the summer I worked on another large (8 x 2½ x 1½ft, 2.4 x 0.8 x 0.5m) section of beech at Ardess Craft Centre. This very sound tree was blown over in a storm in the nearby village of Kesh, and it was wonderful to work on such a large piece of wood with only one small area of rot at the back which, after finishing the carving, I filled with a mix of sawdust and PVA.

I made another tall female figure, this time incorporating a wide base, with a high waist and a relief pattern of diamonds on the dress. I also carved a bird mask, from another piece of the same tree, which was shaped to fit over the head and locate on her tall hair bun. I am letting this piece dry slowly outside to avoid some of the splitting and after a few months I will paint and finish it.

Now I am working on a fourth tall female figure in elm at the workshop. This is a fairly straightforward carving, but will have a wooden cage over the head with four small bird/human figures perched on top of it. I plan to exhibit this along with three or four new sculptures and a new series of woodcut prints. ●

The further I sawed into the trunk the more obvious the rot in the middle became. Once I had finished most of the shaping the whole piece started to split in half. I removed all the soft wood and then made two holes through the torso joining the piece back together with two lengths of screwbar.

I was left with a triangular gap in the dress, and I covered this with two pieces of roofing lead cut to shape and held in place with fencing staples. In a way, this added another dimension to the piece, as it looked as though her dress had been ripped and then patched.

The frames were made separately with small symbols carved on them using a V-shaped woodcut tool, painted and then fitted into the hands. I soaked the base of the sculpture in wood preservative, and after painting and varnishing, it was exhibited in Belfast and now stands in the grounds of Ardess.

Jackie McNamee was born in Belfast and studied sculpture at Edinburgh College of Art. Since graduating she has been based at the Edinburgh Sculpture Workshop and has exhibited her woodcarvings, woodcut prints and drawings in Scotland and Ireland. She has worked as sculptor-in-residence at Ardess Craft Centre in Kesh, Co Fermanagh, for two summers and received an award from the Maypole Fund which enabled her to buy her treasured chainsaw. Jackie can be contacted at the Edinburgh Sculpture Workshop, 25 Hawthornvale, Edinburgh EH6 4JT. Tel: 0131 551 4490

A QUIZZICA

TOM DARBY

The works of Geoff and Hedley Neil have a distinct and sometimes disturbing quality.

Tom Darby was a teacher of industrial arts in New South Wales for 20 years, specialising in woodwork, technical drawing and engineering science. He was subsequently appointed deputy principal of a Central Coast high school before becoming an Inspector of Schools in industrial arts in 1975, being responsible for curriculum development and teacher in-service. On his retirement in 1987, he changed direction and, with his wife Margaret, opened a business, Baringa Woodcrafts. He now designs and makes custom-built furniture.

Tom's book *Making Fine Furniture*, published recently by GMC Publications, features 12 of Australia's finest woodworkers, each of whom has contributed a unique step-by-step project. It is available in Australia from Capricorn Link Pty, 20 Barcoo Street, East Roseville, NSW 2069. Tel: 02 417 6566.

'Hey Mike, come look at this, it's unreal!' Mike and his wife introduced me to the work of Geoff and Hedley Neil. I was at the National Woodworking Exhibition in Melbourne in 1988 and that call to Mike brought others to look at a wood sculpture depicting a giant pair of shears cutting draped fabric. Thrice life size it was eye-catching, but it was the detail that was startling. So startling that you wondered if it really was what you supposed it to be. The fold in the fabric was real; the crease formed ahead of the blade gave the certainty that the scissors were in the process of cutting the material; the junction of the blade and handle as if it had been surface ground; the screw head in the pivot was perfectly turned and the manufacturer's name was 'stamped' on the blade with minute precision. This was abstracted reality and my reaction was quite bizarre.

I can remember standing before that exhibit thinking: 'Hold on, there has to be a glitch somewhere here. Something I can find out of order. Some observation of the original not faithfully translated into wood.' There wasn't and I have since seen many more of Hedley and Geoff Neil's works and each time had the same feeling of incredulity.

It's not only the faithful reproduction which is interesting. Here are two wood sculptors with a wicked sense of humour.

Blue gums in the Watagan Mountains, Central Coast, New South Wales

Like great cartoonists they can bring a smile to your face while making a social comment, leading you to ponder deeper things. Imagine a full-sized pumpkin carved in silky oak. Gnarled, it bears the blemishes of the open field with cheeks and jowls of aged acne. A key protrudes from the ignition switch embedded in the withered end of the strong, virile stem atop the pumpkin. Attached to the key ring are three credit cards which are as believable as every other part of the sculpture - all in wood. The title: '12.01, 1 January 1990'.

For representing fabric they carve from jelutong, a timber with featureless grain which can become towelling or satin depending on their whim. 'Nude' is an old wooden chair. On the back hangs a silk blouse. You know it is sheer and silk. You can almost feel the softness of the fabric as you follow the deep gentle folds running the full length from shoulder to hem. The bodice has been slightly gathered at its top edge, each stitch clearly visible. The buttons hang at odd angles, distorting the fabric into minute folds where they are stitched. The hem is erratic, folding under and out as fine hems on silk do. Folded on the seat of the chair is a denim skirt with a pair of sheer lace edged panties lying on top. How can I detail these materials? It is the carving of the smallest feature in the garment. I'm usually not interested in clothes, but this carving is so real it compels you to look closer to find why it is so.

Reproducing the everyday is not unique. René Magritte has used everyday objects as an art form, but there is a quizzical commentary in all the Neils' work which is unique for wood sculptors. Consider 'Unknown Soldier': a helmet with natural features in the timber forming the bottom lip and shrapnel marks marking the fate of its owner. Daisies rise virulent from the helmet - when will they, ever learn, when will they, ever learn? Or 'Revenge', a five foot high column of steel being felled by a chainsaw, carved in wood. It would be a worthy centrepiece for the next Conservation Foundation conference.

A section of log, bark intact, forms the box from which toilet tissues protrude, as if being dispensed direct from their source

Revenge, Geoff Neil, detail, cedar and steel, life-size

LLOOK AT LIFE

Studio Hi-fi, detail, found object and jelutong, Hedley Neil, life-size

against a wall and then used it as a repository for what must be to hand, could relate directly to this piece.

Many of the Neils' pieces are now in the collections of major Australian corporations. Arnotts, synonymous with biscuits in this country, own a composition called Morning Tea, which features some of Arnotts' most memorable biscuits, sitting on a stump with a mug of tea, an axe and a chisel. Fletcher Jones, the makers of woollen clothes, now use Hedley Neil's shears for promotion. No doubt there are many more corporations who will recognise the value of a corporate carving by the Neils.

Unveiling Pine, Geoff Neil (8¼″ x 13¾″ x 31″ 210mm x 350mm x 780mm)

with the title of 'Bless You'. Once again the detailing is so precise that the realism catches you unawares. The lip of the box is perfectly formed and the tissues, carved from jelutong, are draped as only ultra-light paper can. 'Studio Hi-Fi' is a step ladder, worn and grey, on which the tools and materials of a day's work in the home are deposited. A transistor radio on the top step, the discarded cardigan, tools and glue bottle. Anyone who has leant a ladder

The brothers, Geoff and Hedley, live with their family in Martinsville, at the foot of the Watagan Mountains, inland from Newcastle and, until they establish a gallery close to their workshop, they exhibit in galleries and at exhibitions in Sydney and Newcastle. I recently watched a television interview with a leading Australian cartoonist and was struck by the mannerisms and traits which were similar to those of Geoff and Hedley Neil. Both are quietly spoken and, although conversations are mostly serious, you are often left wondering if you should have listened more carefully. The sparkle in their eye, wry smile and considered understatement suggests there was more to their meaning than you have grasped. Which is undoubtedly a character of their sculpture as well as speech.

I look forward to taking friends to the Neils' exhibitions. If they know nothing about woodwork or sculpture there is always something which catches their imagination and sets them thinking, which ensures lively conversation on the way home. For the serious woodworker, there is always the puzzle, how do they do it? ■

SECOND CHANCES

Trained as a stonemason, Don Rankin has made a successful second career as a sculptor. Here he talks about his latest work

Although I have created sculptures in many parts of the UK as well as in the USA, Canada and Finland, this project in Hornchurch Country Park in Essex was the first time I'd worked near home. In fact the place used to be a playground of mine during the war.

Then it was a Battle of Britain fighter base, Hornchurch Aerodrome. I would have been nine or ten years old and used to go to watch the Spitfires landing and taking off. I saw many aircraft dog-fighting in the air above my home, and in those days of course if you saw a German aircraft come down you cheered, without thinking that there were human beings inside.

War memorial

When I first looked at the site with the idea of creating a sculpture there, I suddenly remembered something I had seen as a child. Once when I approached the boundary fence there was what appeared to be a huge black finger pointing into the sky. When I got nearer I realised it was actually a Dornier bomber that had crash landed on the aerodrome. The fuselage had burnt out and the wing was being propped up in the air by the wheel so it looked like a giant finger. As I'm sure you can see, there is an echo of those images in the work.

The sacrificial piece in the centre is not intended as a monument but to remind us of the

plate rather like an altar – although there is no religious significance to it at all. Five trees were chosen because the site is known as FiveWays, and because five is the minimum needed to create a circle (three would be a triangle and four a square). There are connotations of stone circles, and of course the circle is eternal.

Waste not

All the trees were street trees that were either damaged, rotten or had to come down for some reason or another and would eventually have been burnt or left to rot. I started using reclaimed materials – or giving them a second chance if you like – when I first went to art college in my mid-forties, having worked as a stonemason and landscape gardener most of my life.

young pilots who died, and those who managed to escape from the wreckage but who were horrifically burnt. Those young men gave us a second chance of life. If it weren't for their efforts in the early days of the war, history would have been written in a completely different way.

> # I like the notion that ultimately nature will reclaim the materials I've used... that they will melt into their environment

Even when I think about it, I get a lump in my throat, because – without celebrating war – it is so important for us never to forget the horror of those events.

Called Second Chance, the sculpture consists of five trees around a central beech

Axe man

Tools used were a chainsaw to start with, to remove pieces that were obviously not part of the finished work, and a hand axe. I do a great deal of work with a hand axe, and mine is like a razor. It's a really good tool once you get used to using it – quite punishing on the wrists but nevertheless excellent for the work I do. The only other tool I used was a 1¼in, 32mm gouge; I like to make sure that the gouge marks also work with the rhythms of the wood grain.

> ## It is not intended as a monument, but to remind us of the young pilots who died. Those young men gave us a second chance of life

Top
Gouge marks were intended to work with the rhythms of the wood grain

Above
Burning the outsides was symbolic, but was also meant to encourage moss and lichen to grow on the wood, so nature would reclaim it

For the first time I realised how much material I had produced in my lifetime as a mason, with the chippings and the dust. So I decided to do the same thing – go towards an image in the material, but save all the chippings and the dust. And that's how I got into the notion of reusing materials that had been discarded or were going to be destroyed.

When the trees came into the yard I decided to strip off the bark and leave the natural shapes and forms of the tree for the bottom half. For the upper half I didn't want to carve anything with any sort of figurative quality, but again to respect the natural form of the wood. Where I found that the wood was making spiral or twisting movements they have been faithfully followed in the carving of the upper parts. Even to the point that I have left the flat cut edge where the tops were cut off so that people were aware that they had just been chopped.

All the outside of the trees were burnt. One of the reasons for this is that it will encourage lichen and mosses to develop on the wood, which is part of the work. I like the notion that ultimately nature will reclaim the materials I've used, or that they gradually melt into their environment.

It is a rather strange piece anyway. Close up it's not that big and yet the further away you get, the larger it seems: it has a sort of perspective in reverse.

Final stages

Fixing was done with three stainless steel rods, for which holes had been drilled into the base of each of the trunks, and there is 18in, 450mm of stainless steel embedded into concrete, which was eventually covered with grass. Now it's finished it does look as though the trees grew where they are, with one exception of course, the beech plate in the centre. Beech has a very flat root system. It's from a fallen tree again, of course, so we had it brought here and it's been burnt and drilled to take the stainless steel rods and then turned upside-down, so in fact the roots are exposed.

The two leading trees face exactly south, the finger post at the rear faces exactly north, and the triangulation of the beech plate root also fans towards the south. The shadows cast are quite interesting, although unfortunately there is a signpost in the way, and a bench but this will eventually be moved.

Hands-on learning

The project was sponsored by the London Arts Board, London Borough of Havering and Thames Chase Community Forest. It was the first time the Borough of Havering had commis-sioned a sculptor, and part of my brief was to work with local schoolchildren. Partly I was showing them how to take things from nature to create form, but also explaining something about the natural world – a combination of sculpture and environmental studies.

It should not be surprising that youngsters of this generation who are brought up in towns and cities have little or no knowledge of the environment. Yet I never cease to be amazed at their lack of knowledge when I've taken them into the park. When I asked one child what a particular tree was, he replied – an acorn tree. Well you could say that was pretty close, but he had no idea that the acorn was the seed of the oak.

Children do have environmental education at school but there is nothing like seeing a tree and touching it, rather than looking at a photo-graph or a televised image of it. There is no substitute for hands-on experience, whether it be for sculpture or anything else.

Adopting the work

Since the work was completed, it seems to have become a meeting place for young people. And there are one or two inscriptions of people's names. I don't dislike that, it's as though they're putting a little of themselves on the work. After all it's OK for the artist to go there and make a piece of sculpture in their park, without even asking them if they're happy about it. If they adopt it as belonging to them, then that for me is what the work is about. To me, Second Chance is one of the best pieces of sculpture I have ever made and I feel really proud of it. I don't often get that feeling. ■

Raised in Essex, Don Rankin left school at 14 to train as a stonemason, and for over 20 years ran his own masonry and landscape gardening business. In 1976 he took a foundation arts course, and despite his dyslexia, successfully completed a BA in sculpture at the Central School of Art and Design and an MA in Landscape and Environmental Studies at the Royal College. Since then he has exhibited widely, and worked and lectured in the UK and abroad

ANCIENT & MODERN

Peter Boex talks about the challenges for a contemporary carver working in a medieval style

Heritage agent, and after discussions I developed my design for the new purlins.

This had elements of the fern leaf designs from different examples in the roof, and one new element – a honeysuckle motif which flows through the new designs, not only for the purlins but also in the wallplate and one of the bosses.

Few visitors to the newly restored St Brevitas Church at Lanlivery, near Bodmin in Cornwall, will be aware that some of the medieval carving in the vaulted wooden roof is in fact contemporary.

The £300,000 plus costs of restoring this fourteenth century Grade I listed building, designated as being of outstanding historical and architectural interest, was largely underwritten by English Heritage. This was the largest grant they had ever made to an English parish church.

Carving in a naïve medieval style is difficult for two reasons. First you must downgrade the quality of chisel technique and surface finish; second the design style is more robust and less descriptive than modern carving.

Six bosses of very different designs, 16m of wallplate and five purlins were commissioned. Work started on the purlins for the vaulted roof first, using lengths of English oak 1000 x 150 x 125mm, 40 x 6 x 5in. An original example from the roof was provided by the English

Above
Restored roof to St Brevitas church. The centre line of purlins is new
Below
Original purlin, left, and the newly carved version

Above and left
Peter Boex's design for a new purlin incorporating a honeysuckle motif. It was transferred freehand on to the wood, to give an authentic irregular look

Top left
Boss designed by architect Gordon Collins, with four bells in a cross

Bottom left
Boss incorporating the English Heritage symbol and the date, to acknowledge their sponsorship of the project

Top right
For this boss, Peter Boex had a free hand with the design. It depicts animals and the honeysuckle motif used on purlins

Bottom right
Depiction of the coat of arms of the Duke of Cornwall is strictly regulated, so there was no room for interpretation

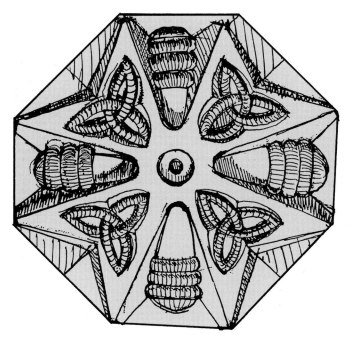

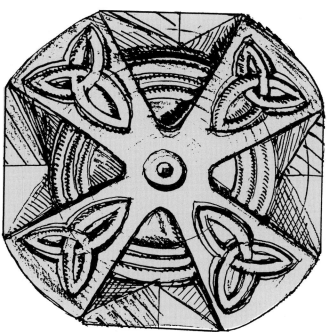

Top
Celtic cross with ropes, designed by Gordon Collins
Above
Second design by Gordon Collins, based on a Celtic cross with rings

Restoration projects involve communication between agent, foreman, builder, workshop carpenter and client

Thinking back

So that a comparable finish to the original carving could be achieved, I tried to put myself into the mind of a journeyman carver of the time. Though this was of course pure fantasy, it did give me a feeling for the work. I imagined having only a few tools, working in the open or a rudimentary shelter, working more from intuition than an elaborate design. More than this, I tried thinking of the carving itself and its long-term future, above the immediate short-term result.

To start the carving on the purlins, the oak balk had to have the edges on one side planed off, so that in end section the top half was semi-round. The carving was incised onto these two rounded edges. The lower half of the balk is uncarved and is embedded upside-down in the ceiling.

Bold designs

The design was drawn onto the wood, freehand, making equal measurements and drawing by eye, not with a template. Looking at the old pieces, none of the elements of patterns are the same size, so I feel this is an authentic technique that gives individuality to the carving.

I used this method of laying out throughout the project, and for some of my own work. After all, when carving you must have the design in your mind, as all guidelines are soon eroded.

All the carving is in more or less deep relief, so there is little scope for modelling the surface and the final appearance depends on the design and the outline.

Good carving depends on experience: you must have done a lot to know a lot. You need to be bold and approach your work with fluidity and confidence. Oak is an especially hard and difficult wood to carve. It responds to bold designs and of course will last for a thousand years. One of its disadvantages is that it shakes and splits along the grain, which can make carving with the grain difficult.

Simple techniques

I began carving the purlins with a ½in v-tool and a heavy mallet, following the outside edge of my design lines. Then I worked up to these lines, cutting across the grain, first with the ⅜in fluted gouge, then the 1in and ¾in flatter gouges in turn, finishing with a flat gouge worked by hand to leave a tooled finish. A small v-tool was used to clean any small fibres from the inner surfaces.

Five purlins were carved in this way. One other piece was scarfed onto an old purlin and carved in a 'distressed' way, to match the old and worn carving. The final effect when the purlins were replaced and the plasterwork finished and limed was very satisfactory. The carving did not stand out as new or obtrusive, but looked like part of the old ceiling.

Next I tackled the wallplate carving. The timber size was 150 x 75mm, 6 x 3in, and three different lengths were used, 5m, 4m and 2m. I thought that I would be carving onto huge balks of oak, which would originally have been used for the wallplates – pieces of wood 300 x 150mm, 12 x 6in, and of variable lengths which received the roof trusses. However, after discussion it was decided to apply the carved 150 x 75mm, 6 x 3in, pieces to the face of the already embedded wallplate timbers, using stainless steel woodscrews.

The first length was in two parts and incorporated the fern design and different hedgerow animals: a mouse, wren, slowworm, frog, long-tailed tit and a squirrel.

Repeat patterns

Similar tools and design techniques were used for carving the wallplate pieces as I had used for the purlins, but to hold lengths of timber I used G-clamps, gripping onto the side of my workbench. I am not used to repetitive work, so there was a mental adjustment to be made when carving these repetitive patterns.

The second length of wallplate was 4m long and had to fit into a position where the original wallplate had been severely damaged with wet rot. The moulding on this piece is known as Aaron's Rod, and is a medieval design based on the biblical story. A stylised leaf pattern is repeated along the length, with a continuous rod moulding in deep relief running down the middle. I did not attempt to join the old wood onto the new, since this would have meant cutting away some of the original medieval carving.

Six of the best

Next stage of the project was the six bosses. Three of the designs were drawn up by Gordon Collins, a retired architect who lives in Lanlivery. Two of these were based on a Celtic cross motif and the third used a clever design in the shape of a cross using four bells, with bell rope motifs between each.

> # So that a comparable finish could be achieved, I tried to put myself into the mind of a journeyman carver of the time

The fourth boss recorded English Heritage's patronage of the restoration. Their logo and the date were woven into a design using oak leaves and branches.

For the fifth boss I was given a free hand. The design reflects contemporary conservation and environmental concerns, with four animal heads looking down from each corner - a badger, a fox, an owl and a rabbit. The honeysuckle motif used in the purlins and the wallplate was repeated here.

I felt that this design not only embodied medieval principles but also worked in situ, even when seen 20ft up.

Prince Charles, the Duke of Cornwall, funded the final boss, so it shows his coat of arms. No other design features could be included as the representation of the coat of arms is strictly regulated. This carving was more delicate and detailed than the other work, which caused some problems because small raised sections of oak are liable to split away if the chisel is forced. I therefore had to pare with the chisels and work more slowly than if I were using lime, for example.

Restoration projects are not always as straightforward as they seem. They involve communication between agent, foreman, builder, workshop carpenter and client. Along the way, designs, deadlines and personal preferences have to be juggled. In the end it almost seems that the carving itself is a secondary consideration. However, such is the job of a professional carver, and he or she must balance these aspects to fulfil the commission. ∎

Chris Wormald

Born in Australia in 1952, Peter Boex has lived in Cornwall for 20 years. By the time he was 16 he was already carrying out carving commissions for his school, Bradfield College, and local organisations. He is self-taught, but influenced by other contemporary carvers, such as Doug Smith at Silchester, and Faust and Warton Lang in St Ives, as well as medieval and Celtic designs.
Doug Smith once told him: 'If you call yourself a carver, then you should be able to carve anything.' Such for better or worse has been Peter's credo, but he is happiest when developing his own work

Mostyn Kimber's first carvings were a challenge
but they have also brought him much pleasure

Tree Fruits

LUCKY STRIKE

E arly or semi-retirement opens up opportunities for new initiatives. But many of the options lie fallow because of the difficulty in overcoming personal inertia, lack of confidence, or ignorance of appropriate skills.

This was largely true for me and woodcarving because, although captivated by it here and on holiday in Switzerland, it never occurred to me I could aspire to such endeavours. My career had been in aeronautical design with a mathematical background and there were no personal indications of any talent for graphic art or creative crafts.

So it was just by happy chance, at an opportune time, I noticed an advertisement for a local evening class in woodwork which included some woodcarving. There it was, an opportunity to attempt the impossible, without the gamble on the outlay for tools normally incurred.

Full of trepidation, I turned up the first evening at Wheathampstead School where it was suggested I sketch something on a 2 x 6in, 50 x 150mm scrap of wood and start shaping it. It matters little now the teacher was not a renowned woodcarver, nor that the result was virtually a two dimensional oddity.

Early experiences

Mother Love

I was cutting wood, hardly carving, but enjoying it and pleased with the grain patterns I accidentally produced. Over the first term I made progress from a small cat in cherrywood (*Prunus spp*), via a swan in sycamore (*Acer pseudoplatanus*), to a stylised father-daughter figure also in cherry.

This seemed to please the teacher and quite surprised me. I was hooked and felt it safe to make a modest investment in tools and shed space for this engrossing activity.

Over the next few years my involvement with woodcarving was characterised by an obsession for carving in any free time and regular attendance at the evening class. These schools provide a valuable service to local communities. In my case, it was a warm, dry venue where I could meet others with similar interests in woodwork and share experiences.

As well as the carving tools, the equipment included a bandsaw which is a great saver of time and energy for bosting out surplus wood. I learned about tools and their care, about cutting in sympathy with the grain, not cutting my fingers, and about alternative kinds of finishing.

It was a wonderful time providing an outlet for my mental and physical energies, and a whole new interest in life. Almost any wood was worth scrounging, and some even worth buying to try out its workability and visual appeal. I soon found which woods seemed suitable. Despite what can be culled from books, there is nothing to beat personal experience, which sinks in and stays.

Male Head stained, with beeswax finish

My first tools were those already owned, among which were some straight, flat chisels. Strangely, these are the ones I still use often. Even stranger was when later on, I visited the workshops of a leading woodcarving firm in Brienz and noticed more than half the 20 carvers had a straight chisel in their hands. Perhaps it was just straight chisel day.

It would be wrong to suggest it can all be done with straight chisels. A good carving knife, some gouges and fishtails were vital additions to a couple of carver's mallets I made early on in the evening class.

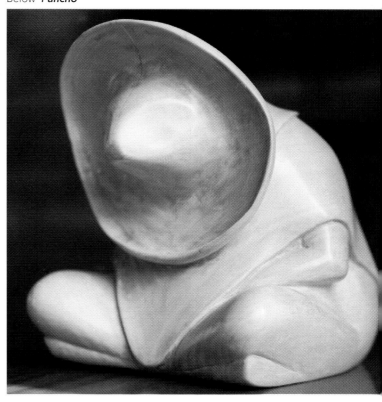

Making headway

With the passage of time the urge to carve at every opportunity subsided and I became more selective about the choice of subject. When I moved to Warwickshire I was able to attend a professional carver's class at the Mid-Warwickshire College at Leamington Spa. Paul Lewis, while down to earth and an advocate of gouge, chisel and mallet rather than machine tools, was quite perceptive in exercising judgement between allowing free reign, or stepping in with advice and practical demonstration.

Under his tutelage it seemed propitious to attempt something I had previously avoided, the carving of a full-size male head, using English oak (*Quercus robur*).

It was a daunting, sometimes humbling experience, and I had awful problems with the mouth. Initially the quite respectable looking closed lips were apparently set too high, so it was suggested the lower lip be removed and re-cut to convey a slightly open mouth with visible teeth.

What a prospect! The lesson I learned was to avoid making statements too soon and when made, they need not always be final. I persevered and eventually finished what was an unmistakable, if imperfect, male head. My wife, and probably others too polite to say so, disliked the carving, especially the mouth which was somewhat horrific, but I found it a valuable experience.

About a year later, having become used to having it around, it seemed worth trying to give it a face-lift, even with the risk of ruining the whole thing. So I re-shaped the lips, this time with upturned, smiley ends, and I added some laughter lines to produce a more pleasant visage.

Subsequently, I have included facial features on other heads but always with some trepidation. Perhaps the old Swiss woodcarvers had a point about the need to confine and specialise your activities to either human or animal subjects.

Even so, I have enjoyed varying the menu, maybe something to do with being a late developer with limited time left to indulge in this absorbing pastime.

Overcoming obstacles

During this phase there were two carvings which were significant for different reasons. The first was *Peasant Woman* for which I incorrectly selected a much-cherished chunk of yew (*Taxus baccata*) from Dorset.

The figure of the grain enhanced the general interest but was wrong for the face where it confused the feature detail. It would probably have been better to use lime or alternatively to have provided a stylised face,

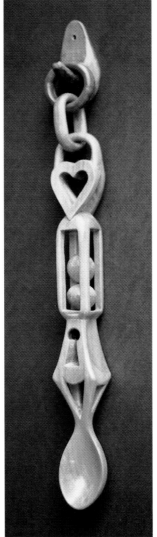

without features, for this attractive yew.

The second carving was an excursion into three dimensional curves and symmetries in the form of a sleepy mexican in sycamore entitled *Pancho*. The choice of wood, and the divergent grain of two pieces glued centrally, enhanced the symmetry. With his overall attitude and dented sombrero, it conveyed my design intention to create a bit of a character.

These two efforts were based on full-size design sketches. The male head had been carved direct, with few guide lines cut into the block and the rest evolving from interaction between mind, hands and tools with the wood.

A complete contrast to these was a Welsh lovespoon incorporating twin-hearts, keyhole, captive spheres and links, all symbolic. The design and fashioning of this in rosewood (*Dalbergia spp*) was a joy, and provided a satisfying heirloom going back to my origins.

Animal appeal

I have continued to progress over the last decade and included the carving of animals and birds. I have never felt compelled to sculpt birds in exact detail, which may reflect my limitations, but have enjoyed producing what I believe are recognisable outcomes for wrens, swans, ducks and one ambitious eagle.

The appeal of the wren, for me, lies in its minuteness and pert attitude which I have attempted to capture, also reluctantly staining to obtain a better result. It was a boost to my morale when my first wren was favourably regarded by an acquaintance of international repute in biology, who persuaded me to sell it to him.

Opposite below left **Kimber's heirloom lovespoon**
Left *Woodland Fragment* and *Pert Wrens*
Below left ***Going for the Kill***
Below ***Jungle Cat***

My early efforts with cedar (*Cedrus spp*) gave delightful aesthetic outcomes and the carving process was enhanced by wafts of its unique aroma when cut. I found it unsuitable, however, for thin cross-sections across grain.

Castello boxwood (*Gossypiospermum praecox*) with its close grain allowed me to use thin sections for tails, fins and wave forms, resulting in clean lines as in *Sea Song*. I made an alternative design in walnut (*Juglans spp*) called *Cresting the Wave*, illustrating the potential of this wood for delicate structure and pleasing aesthetics.

Creative challenges

Now my efforts tend to be in two distinct categories, abstract/stylised designs including three dimensional figures, and relief carvings. These are complete contrasts. The former allows creative freedom which extends into the process of carving, whereas the latter demands fairly precise interpretation and accurate representation of design sketches.

Black Gold is a directly carved abstract in African blackwood (*Dalbergia melanoxylon*), pleasing to handle and with visually interesting patterns which, allied to its shape and colour, are reminiscent of iron pyrites seen in irregular lumps of coal.

Lady in a cloak and *Mother Love* both in yew, are typical of my stylised figure abstracts with consideration of heart and sapwood to enhance the outcomes.

Blithe Spirits in beechwood (*Fagus sylvatica*) was a theme in which mother and child figures were used in an attempt to capture the exhilaration of carefree dance. The carving of abstracts engenders for me an extra affinity with wood and a natural interaction between mind and subject, which seems to facilitate its evolution.

I did not attempt relief carving earlier because of low confidence in my ability to draw free-hand and uncertainty about setting about relief subjects.

Paul Lewis helped me to produce a small

At the other end of the scale, was the eagle in mahogany (*Swietenia spp*) with a 14in, 355mm wing span, called *Going for the Kill*. This was a challenge and demanded I include feather detail. To safeguard the delicate wing tips I mounted it on an oval plaque in ponderosa pine (*Pinus ponderosa*).

Animals have been a different and difficult medium for expression and range from the humble mouse via the household cat to a prowling jungle cat in West African padauk (*Pterocarpus soyauxii*), which slowly turned from rich red to black over time.

The slender legs revealed the need for consideration of short grain effects, or selective orientation of the run of the grain, to prevent catastrophic fracture during the carving. This was where my engineering background should have forewarned me, but I ignored it to my cost. However, repairs were possible and I learned another lesson about the behaviour of wood.

Dolphins have featured in my carvings and have been a fertile field for original design, exploring woods and revealing differences in final grain pattern.

grapevine cluster on a panel of afrormosia (*Pericopsis elata*), not a good wood for carving. The learning curve was steep and the approach of Easter inspired me to extend the theme, this time on my own, on a more suitable plank of beech a few feet long.

After some research in the local library I drew, to my surprise, a credible sketch of an ascending array of grapes and vine leaves as a guide to my carving. The work was a challenge but surprisingly utterly relaxing and the finished relief, stained to a darker colour, seemed to invite the title *The True Vine*.

Acting on a suggestion, I offered it to our local church to hang in the new church hall. This was a carving I enjoyed immensely and an outcome I would never have predicted.

Subsequent relief work included a river scene *The Swans of Avon*, a woodland fragment called *Wrens* (a commemoration), and a triptych in natural beech which I have named *Three Fruits*. It consists of three panels depicting grapes, crab apples and acorns.

My most recent relief carving is *Rough Seam*, in stained sycamore. The motivation for this came from a long standing desire to pay tribute through my work to my father and other relatives, with a history of noble endeavour in Welsh coal mining.

The final impetus came from the closing of the last coal mine in the Rhymney Valley at Penallta where I was born and brought up. The relief depicts work in a low and rough seam, and was derived in part from a cartoon by Steve Bell, the well-known cartoonist, published the morning after three miners lost their lives under a roof-fall in Bilsthorpe Colliery.

Woodcarving has exerted influence on my life beyond anything I might have envisaged and significantly changed my attitude towards things hitherto taken for granted. Paintings and works of art in china, pottery, metal and wood

Left **Rough Seam**
Below left **Blithe Spirits**
Right **The True Vine**

were regarded in a new light, often with mental assessment of their suitability for re-interpretation as subjects for carving.

Trees have been a fascination for me since boyhood but carving has provided new insights into the unique qualities wood derives from natural growth and how it lends itself to transformation into objects of beauty.

Every carving is a challenge and, in the experimental phase, each was for me a voyage into the unknown, travelling more in hope than certainty. Achievement of even a fair outcome with a new subject represented the scaling of a personal peak, and some were milestone events leading to increased confidence and wider scope.

The interaction with people has been an unexpected pleasure. Conversations range from the fairly trivial to the deeply moving, when a stranger confides a personal sorrow as the reason for a particular carving or special commission.

Woodcarving seems to offer a medium for all levels of ability with scope for an infinite variety of outcomes. When I see the best examples, in exhibitions or magazines like **Woodcarving**, I am filled with awe and admiration for the carvings and their originators and have a strong urge to give up and put away my tools forever.

On reflection I realise not everyone is able to scale the Himalayas of carving and there is no reason why I should not continue at a more modest level, if it gives me and sometimes others pleasure.

I am grateful to my mentors and also for the serendipity which brought me to this artistic craft towards the end of my main career. My experience is probably far from unique but may provide some incentive to others who hesitate to pursue new initiatives and may encourage them to have a go. ●

Mostyn Kimber is a chartered engineer who started carving at the end of a career in the aerospace industry. Well known for his commitment to engineering design, he was the founding chairman of SEED (Sharing Experience in Engineering Design) and took up woodcarving as a creative outlet in his mellow years.

STREET STYLE

Colin Wilbourn's sculptures take art out of the gallery and into the streets

Choosing sculpture as a profession was not an easy decision for Colin Wilbourn. He describes his upbringing in Hertfordshire as 'ordinary working class, council house and comprehensive school'. And although his parents encouraged him to take a degree in fine art, he felt guilty. 'With all the social problems, I found myself asking where art fits in today's society.'

His answer has been to work on commissions and residencies for large scale sculptures in public places, 'where the work will be seen and enjoyed by as many people as possible'.

Ideal sites

After completing a BA at Newcastle Polytechnic and an MA at Newcastle University, the North-East of England became Colin's adopted home. One of his first residencies was at Durham Cathedral, where he worked in both stone and wood. For one sculpture, thirteen carved elm trees were used to create the splendid *Upper Room*, featured in **Woodcarving** issue 15.

'It suddenly came home to me how important it is to work on site,' says Colin. 'Probably one of the reasons *The Upper Room* remained unvandalised is that it didn't appear overnight. It took six months to carve, during which time all kinds of people stopped to chat and got involved. It is as if watching it grow gave them an interest, and a respect for the sculpture.'

A sense of place

Colin's CV includes an impressive list of exhibitions and private and public commissions. However, his favourite working method is the residency. Too often, he feels, public art is an optional extra, plonked down in the middle of a space with no reference to the surroundings or the people who live and work there.

With a residency he can get to know the site. 'You absorb all the information unconsciously and it comes back unconsciously in the things you want to make. Inspiration doesn't switch on like a lightbulb; it grows out of a two-way process.'

Right **High Window**, 1993. Copper beech, 35 x 4 x 4ft, 10.7 x 1.2 x 1.2m 'This piece was made for Wydale, the York Diocesan Centre near Scarborough. The 150-year-old tree had lost most of its limbs in a storm, but was still alive. Wydale is often used as a retreat, and to me the carving is about escape, with its ladder and open window. It also has references to the biblical story of Jacob's Ladder, particularly with its slightly dream-like quality. The tree continues to live and grow.'

The Last Supper Table, 1987.
Fumed oak and inlay,
4 x 3 x 3ft, 1.2 x 0.9 x 0.9m
'Completed during my
residency at Durham
Cathedral, this is based on the
theme of the Last Supper and
how that event became
symbolised by the communion
service. The simple carving on
the top representing elements
of the Last Supper is in four
hinged sections which unfold
to reveal an inlaid pattern
symbolising parts of the
Eucharist. Something real and
three-dimensional becomes a
symbolic pattern showing how
a private occasion became a
public ritual.'

However he prefers not to do too much factual research. 'If you do too much you can end up with ideas that are expected. If you don't know enough you can come up with ideas that are unexpected.'

Hidden meanings

This element of the unexpected, the bizarre, is very much a trademark of Colin's work. *The Upper Room* is a masterpiece of *trompe l'oeil*, which must be viewed from one specific point. *Water Log*, a piece commissioned by Scarborough Council, has a jug suspended in mid-air, apparently pouring water into the tree.

In another series of works in Greenhead Park in Huddersfield, slices of domestic life are carved into isolated trees. Sculptures such as *The Last Supper Table* and *Things Fall Apart* have literal and symbolic meanings.

Appropriate materials

Colin often works with reclaimed materials. Many of the wooden sculptures are carved from diseased elms. In his current residency, at the St Peter's Riverside Sculpture Project in Sunderland, he used reclaimed stone to create a carved stair carpet on steps down to the river; and red sandstone from an old bridge went to make The Red House, a part-ruined ground floor of a house, full of furniture and personal possessions – 'like Pompeii or the Marie Celeste'.

Perhaps the most unusual material he has worked with is chocolate. The piece, entitled *After All Chocolate is our Bread and Butter*, was a table laid for tea, with a sliced loaf and butter. Commissioned by Rowntree Macintosh for a travelling exhibition, it had to be remade from the master mould for each venue as visitors kept eating bits of it.

It is a response that would meet with the artist's approval. 'If I can make something that, for just a moment, will intrigue, inspire or give people enjoyment, then that's great.'

Left **Water Log**, 1991.
Elm, 12 x 3 x 3ft,
3.7 x 0.9 x 0.9m
'Carved from a tree
that had died from
Dutch elm disease,
this sculpture
remains, still rooted,
where it grew. It is
next to a busy traffic
island with plenty of
pedestrian access on
The Crescent in
Scarborough. I felt
that it should be
something with a
strong impact, but
that was readily
identifiable, so
passing motorists
would see and
recognise it even
though it is so
incongruous.'

Between Us, 1991.
Elm, 13 x 6 x 4ft,
4 x 1.8 x 1.2m
'A private commission,
by a woman in memory
of her late husband. He
had spent a lot of his
time cultivating some
land as a kind of wildlife
conservation area, and
his main passion had
been trees. Using a
couple of elms that had
fallen in high winds, I
made two chairs of
different styles, sharing
one wavy seat. The
back of each chair
becomes a ladder,
climbing upwards and
joining to form one,
which passes through
an opening in a canopy
of leaves. The sculpture
is sited so that it looks
out over both the valley
that the man cultivated
and the wife's house; in
turn it can be seen from
both these places.'

Colin Wilbourn

Passing Through, 1994. Elm
'This is one of a series of several carvings that I am doing in Greenhead Park in Huddersfield. They have linking themes about domesticity, protective clothing and artefacts. Work is still in progress.'

Things Fall Apart, 1986. Ash, 5.5 x 4 x 4ft, 1.7 x 1.2 x 1.2m
'Often we think we know or understand one another, but sometimes we find that what appear as similarities become differences. The sculpture is a physical manifestation of this. It is a table set as if for breakfast for two, carved from a single trunk of ash. Everything is in its proper place, everything seems all right. But the tensions hidden inside have caused the table to split violently in two. On the split sections are carved two different images representing the people's opposing ideals.'

Ted Jackson tells how a Rolls Royce and falling on hard times led him into a new career as a woodcarver

Just 15 years ago I was earning my living as a general woodworker on the west coast of Scotland. I tackled everything from building work to custom furniture, kitchens to boat repairs, but at this time I was unaware of the wealth of carving talent in Britain. Features in woodworking magazines about carvers were a revelation to me, particularly the work of Ian Norbury, Ray Gonzalez and Les Jewell.

I had no inclination to start carving until I was asked to repair the ash framing on a 1929 Rolls Royce Phantom II car six years ago. This included two support blocks which had to be sculpted to fit the curves of the rear valance. My partner remarked I had made a good job of the blocks and suggested I tried carving something more interesting.

Soon afterwards we moved to Devon, and finding myself with more spare time and a large block of lime (*Tilia vulgaris*) I made a start. I had two second-hand gouges and some assorted knives as well as my existing toolkit and a Workmate.

First work

Inspired by Ian Norbury's first book, I carved a frog sitting on a stylized rock. With beginner's impatience I failed to study the subject closely enough, with the result that although the carving looked like a frog and had some life to it, there were some obvious errors.

However, I liked it enough to continue, and this first attempt was followed by life-size carvings of two lizards, a weasel and another frog, all in lime, and a larger than life size hawk's head in mahogany (*Swietenia macrophylla*).

While my work was steadily improving, it was obvious my tools and equipment were not adequate for more ambitious projects, so I set myself a test. If I did well enough it would be worth investing in better equipment.

Artists and sculptors seem to agree that hands are the most difficult subject to get right, so I attempted a study of my own right hand in fiddleback or rippled sycamore (*Acer pseudoplatanus*). It took three months with much stopping and agonising, but I was pleased with the result and convinced myself and my partner I should improve my tools.

The deepening recession in the building trade meant more carving time and I was faced with more decisions. Was my work good enough to sell? Should I go on a course? What work would sell best? What were the best outlets? How do you price an article of craft and art?

I soon decided against doing a course because of the cost, and also because I did not know what to go for. One carver I knew signed up for a course where the tutor was a sculptor interested only in free expression and abstract work, and who wouldn't or couldn't answer questions on tools, sharpening and basic techniques.

Above **Hawk's head in mahogany**
Right **Dragon in mahogany**
Opposite above **Dolphin in English walnut**
Opposite right **Frog in lime**

By this time my main interest was in carving in the round, and I decided that at the age of 57 I didn't have time to develop the different skills required for other areas of carving. I would concentrate on what I knew and liked best.

Selling work

When it came to selling work, cost considerations ruled out craft fairs and my own workshop/display area. This only left shops and commissions. I went to several art and craft shops in the area and got a positive response from two.

The owner of one shop specialising in wood was helpful. She wouldn't take any of the pieces I showed her, but gave advice on improvements to finish and presentation to make my work more saleable. I took her advice which resulted in my first two sales, and I have sold repeatedly through this shop since.

One piece was a duck in yew (*Taxus baccata*) and a second, also in yew, was shown to a woman interested in my work who bought it on the spot. This led, by word of mouth, to other commissions and I now spend about three quarters of my working week carving.

Experience shows that animals and wildlife sell best, but not all of it. Birds seem to be universally popular, particularly ducks, and I have been successful with frogs and lizards on various bases.

Dolphins and whales are popular but there is strong competition from these made in other materials. They are also difficult to present, as a leaping dolphin, its tail lost in a stylized wave, looks unbalanced to me. One answer was to mount the carving on a rock to represent the animal swimming in its natural environment.

Cats, otters and pigs are popular, but dogs and horses are usually commissioned by people wanting studies of their pets. I had no response to a terrapin in padauk (*Pterocarpus spp.*) yet a loggerhead turtle in English walnut (*Juglans regia*) sold within a month.

There was strong reaction to my carved hand. Some loved it, others were repelled by it, and one woman refused to touch it. Four shops told me to take it to an art gallery.

Pricing

Pricing has been the biggest problem, especially when carving on spec. Commissions are more straightforward, as you agree a subject and price with your client and are then both committed to it. There can still be problems, but at least you know what you are aiming for. Costing a piece you hope will attract a chance buyer is another matter.

As I am still inexperienced I spend a lot of time on waste removal and overcoming problems. If I included all this time in my final pricing it would make it prohibitive, so for now I have evolved a rather haphazard process of deciding what I think I can get for a carving. This is often unsatisfactory in terms of an hourly rate for my labour, but I expect it to improve as I become more confident and am able to further improve my equipment.

I have already started to speed things up by increasing my collection of gouges and by designing and building a carving stand with a 4in, 100mm swivelling vice bolted on. This was cheap as it was made mainly from scrap wood. It works well and is certainly a big improvement on using only the Workmate.

Sharpening with an oilstone was time consuming, so after much discussion with other carvers and reading of magazine articles I bought a bench grinder, reversed and fitted with a hard felt wheel. Once I found the right buffing compound I was able to get a razor sharp edge in seconds.

Choosing tools

Choosing carving tools has been interesting. An old Sheffield carbon steel carving knife which had been my grandfather's, takes a fine edge and holds it for months, freshened with a steel occasionally. Second-hand Addis, Herring and Buck Bros gouges seem to be made of similar material.

I have bought new gouges from seven manufacturers and am sorry to say the best ones are Swiss and Austrian. British made ones don't hold an edge as well and are too thick in the shaft for me. But so far I have bought only one gouge which has proved to be virtually useless.

I also have several knives, particularly for fine detail work. Some of these I ground for a particular job and then found I continued to use them for other jobs. I have to be careful as I like tools and it would be easy for me to build up a large collection of fancy gouges which would hardly ever be used.

Timbers

Like most carvers, I started with lime. I had a large block which lasted a good time and produced five carvings. I next tried mahogany which had a difficult counter grain but on which it was easy to get a good finish.

I tried padauk, only once. It splintered badly, the end grain crumbled and it was difficult to polish. The only thing I liked about it was the colour. A block of air dried sycamore was very hard but cut cleanly and took good detail.

When hobby carving I chose a subject to suit the wood I had handy. When carving to sell you have to take the opposite approach, and finding suitable blocks for the chosen subject is more difficult. I try to plan ahead and call at timber stores when passing on visits to friends and family.

I usually call at John Boddy's Fine Wood and Tool Store in Yorkshire, and Yandles in Somerset when I can, and I have a good local supplier in John Bradford who usually has good air dried timber in heavy section.

With some pieces I have tried to enhance the carving by using timber with striking grain. Yew, sweet chestnut (*Castanea sativa*) and cherry (*Prunus spp.*) have given good results. I have recently tried wych elm (*Ulmus glabra*) and tulipwood (*Dalbergia frutescens*).

I have had difficulty finding English walnut in big enough pieces, and prices vary considerably. I eventually

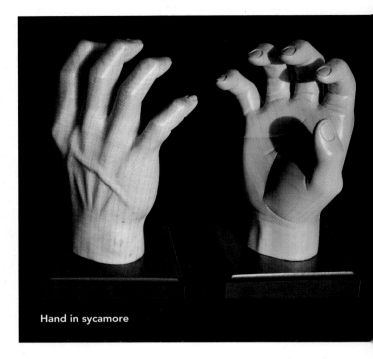

Hand in sycamore

bought a block by mail order and got a lovely piece of wood, but I much prefer to see what I am buying.

Finishing

A good finish is vital. I have seen good carvings spoilt by poor sanding and unsuitable varnishes. I don't like varnish or lacquer on woodcarvings so I have experimented with oils. Boiled linseed oil turns lime yellow and takes too long to dry, and teak oil needs up to eight coats to get a gloss and tends to be patchy.

I have now discovered Blackfriars Scandinavian oil. Two or three coats, thinned with a little white spirit, soaks into the grain and dries in four to six hours, both feeding and sealing the wood. As a final finish I apply wax polish, rubbing down the first coat with fine wire wool.

I am never fully satisfied with my work and my chief inspector even less so. She merely points a finger and lifts an eyebrow and it's back to the carving stand for me. On the other hand it's a big boost to your ego when total strangers admire your work enough to buy it. Even though I'm not making a fortune, it's much more interesting than making timber frames for houses.

Do you believe in destiny or is life a series of random events? My move to Scotland, working on the Rolls Royce, then moving to Devon and finding work short were all chance events through which I discovered a hidden talent and embarked on a new career which is certainly enjoyable and won't make me retire at 65. ●

Second hand carving tools:
Bristol Design, 14 Perry Road, Bristol BS1 5BG
Tel: 0117 929 1740
Timber supplies:
John Boddy's Fine Wood and Tool Store,
Riverside Sawmills, Boroughbridge, N.Yorks YO5 9LJ
Tel: 01423 322370
Yandle & Sons Ltd,
Hurst Works, Martock, Somerset TA12 6JU
Tel: 01935 822207

VICTORIAN VENTURER

T he name of 19th century woodcarver James Elwell may not be familiar to those outside the picturesque market town of Beverley, East Yorkshire, where Elwell lived and worked for more than 70 years. But examples of his work can be found in places as diverse as Lincoln Cathedral and Sydney Town Hall, Australia.

Born in Perry Barr, a suburb of Birmingham in 1836, Elwell moved to Beverley at the age of 13, when his father became involved with the construction of the local railway line.

After serving an apprenticeship with a local company of cabinet makers, Elwell went to London to find work. He returned to Beverley in the 1860s, and became foreman of a firm of cabinet makers and upholsterers, situated next to Beverley's last remaining medieval gateway, the North Bar. He eventually took over and, at the height of his success, employed 60 craftsmen.

Gothic screen

Elwell's first major commission was in 1877, when he was recommended to the architect Sir George Gilbert Scott, who

Above *The Political Cheap Jack*, the carving over the door of number six, depicts Disraeli as a travelling salesman, willing to sacrifice Liberal policies for more votes. On each side are figures of John Bull and his dog (right) and a kilted Scotsman
Left Detail of John Bull and his dog (left) and an unknown man playing a musical instrument

Madeleine Wolf documents the career of
James Elwell, a 19th century Yorkshire carver
whose work reached as far as Australia

was working on the restoration of Beverley's large Gothic Minster. Elwell sent him a small example of his work, and this helped to persuade Scott the local woodcarver was as skilled as any of the more well-known London companies to carry out the prestigious commission.

Elwell was asked to carve a new oak (*Quercus robur*) choir screen to Scott's design, based on the existing 16th century choir stalls. In the medieval period Beverley had been an important centre for the Northern Guild of Minstrels. As a result, both the town's main churches contained numerous carvings of medieval musicians and their instruments. The new choir screen continued this musical theme.

Standing 27ft, 8.2m high, the screen was supported by four carved columns. In the niches were 16 statues of figures connected with music. Among them were King David with his harp, the Emperor Charlemagne, known for his interest in the arts and founding several singing schools, and Emperor Constantine who supposedly developed a new method of chanting.

Above ***Will they work?*** **The carving over number eight depicts Gladstone as a hunter, straining to hold the leashes of four dogs, each representing a different political party**

On the rear of the screen were several carved figure-heads holding musical instruments, imitating the style of the earlier medieval carved figures dotted about the church. The oak choir screen took three years to complete at a cost of £3,300. For the first year or so Elwell worked alongside his six craftsmen for 10–12 hours a day.

Church commissions

Apart from receiving universal acclaim for the finished screen, it made Elwell's name as an ecclesiastical woodcarver and gave him many other commissions for work in churches around Britain.

These included stall work in Lincoln Cathedral and Bakewell Church, Derbyshire, and screens for St Agnes church in Kennington and Holy Trinity church, Hull among others.

He also worked on the reredos, the ornamental screen behind the altar, and the choir screen in St Mary's Beverley,

Above left **Two of the carved statues in front of the choir screen, depicting St Cecilia patron saint of musicians, and Caedmon, a seventh century poet and musician**
Above **The oak choir screen in Beverley Minster, James Elwell's first commission**

designed by John Oldrid Scott, son of Sir George Gilbert.

A major overseas commission for Elwell was to design the carved case for the organ in Sydney Town Hall, or Centennial Hall as it was named when it opened in 1889.

At the time, it was said to be the largest town hall in the world, containing one of the largest musical organs, a title it still retains. Carving the organ case was no small task for an instrument boasting six keyboards, 127 stops and 8,672 pipes.

Tudor facades

In 1880, Elwell worked on number 43 North Bar Without, Beverley, known as Oak House. The exterior was in his trademark mock-Tudor black and white with a carved, wooden front door. Interior fixtures included an oak carved balustraded staircase, carved internal doors, parquet flooring and ornate dining room fireplace, overlaid in a fruit and leaf design, complete with classical Ionic columns.

Four years later Elwell turned his attention to number 45, known as Pinewood, this was also given a mock-tudor facade. Over the front door with its leaded glass panes, Elwell carved a scene from a story by Dickens called *The Cricket and the Hearth*.

J.L Toole a comedian friend of Elwell's had recently taken part in a London stage production of the story. The scene shows Toole in his role of the old toy maker Caleb Plummer working on a wooden horse. Underneath is his phrase "We like to go as near as nature as we can for sixpence." Among his interior work here was a Queen Anne style fireplace.

As Elwell's woodcarving business expanded he was able to buy two neighbouring properties, numbers six and eight, North Bar Without. These he demolished and rebuilt in 1892–94 giving them mock-Tudor facades which incorporated examples of his skill as a craftsman.

He included several small carved figures. Among them John Bull, a Scotsman and a sneering woman. Perched next to

the turret of number eight Elwell inserted the small, cheeky, red-coloured figure of a devil, known locally as old Nick.

On the front of number 4, his family home, he placed three painted figures, one of which remains. It is thought to represent St John the Evangelist, the patron saint of Beverley Minster.

Political scenes

Over two of the doorway lintels political scenes based on Punch cartoons were carved. They were created in 1892 by one of Elwell's employees, W.J Thornley, to his specifications.

The carving at number 6, entitled *The Political Cheap Jack* depicts Disraeli as a travelling salesman addressing a crowd of workers from a covered wagon. He holds two pieces of paper, the smaller represents Liberal policies which he is prepared to throw away in order to gain the popular vote, illustrated by the larger piece of paper in his left hand.

The carving over number eight, called *Will They Work?* shows Gladstone dressed for a shooting party, struggling to hold the leashes of four dogs straining in different directions. They each represent political parties with their own views on the question of Home Rule for Ireland.

When Elwell eventually retired, he handed over the running of his business to two of his sons, John and Edward. He died in 1926 aged 90, leaving his sons to carry on the business. This they did for many more years, although sadly the woodcarving side disappeared.

Despite this, James Elwell will not be forgotten thanks to the legacy of fine craftsmanship he left in Beverley and many other places both in this country and abroad. ●

Index

A

advertising	19
ageing wood	52
animals	107-8
selling	115
antique effects	51-4
approaches to work *see* working methods	
axes	100
Ayers, Bob	17-19

B

baskets	58-9
beech (*Fagus sylvatica*)	65
Beesley, Alicia	27-31
birds	37, 59, 107-8
selling	115
Boex, Peter	102-5
bosses	102-5
boxes	58-9
Brennan, Ian	2-5
Bullard, Stan	41-5
burning	
for effect	75
to age wood	52
to encourage lichen and mosses	100
burrs, elm	10-11
businesses *see* small businesses	

C

Caink, Richard	74-8
caricatures *see* figures	
carving	
see also relief carving	
historical development	88-9
medieval style	102-5
process *see* working methods	
Victorian	114-19
chainsaws	8, 64, 77, 93
Cloutier, Pier	55-7
colouring	65, 89
and commercialism	90
commercialism	90
contour	88
costing *see* pricing	
cracks	8, 28, 65, 83
plugging	31
Cress, Jake	68-70
crowns and crests	2-5

D

Darby, Tom	96-7
Décorse, Pierre	20-3
Deschênes, Benoi	55-7
duplicators	54

E

elm (Ulmus spp)	65-6
burrs	10-11
Elwell, James	117-19

environment *see* nature	
exhibitions, *Echoes in the Landscape*	12, 16

F

fabric, carving	96
Fearnhead, Jonathan	79-83
feathers	60
figures	46-9, 71-3
humour in	24-6
mythological	79-83
religious	6-9
finishing	58, 83, 116
see also patinas	
large sculptures	9, 22, 67, 94
fixing, sculpture	100
folk art	51-4
Foster, Hugh	17-19
Freeze, Lori	46-9
fruit woods	66
Fuetsch, Anton	88-91
furniture	49, 68-70
as sculpture	44-5, 77-8

G

Gertner, Zoë	58-60
gouges	60, 82
large sculptures	8, 100

H

Hare, Jim	27-31
Harrison, Ed	10-11
heartwood, and sapwood	58, 60
historical development, of carving	88-9
Hodges, Harriet	68-70
humour	
figures	24-6, 46-9
furniture	68-70
large sculpture	23

I

inspiration	9, 24-5, 43, 71
motherhood	92-5
mythology	79-83
nature and landscape	12-16, 23
religion	6

J

Jackson, Ted	114-16
Jakes, Robert	61-3
jelutong	96, 97
Johnson, Carl	24-6

K

Kimber, Mostyn	106-9

L

laminating	32-3, 82-3
landscape, inspirational source	12-16
Langan, Tom	50-4

Latham, Simon   6-9
Lee, Les   84-7
lime (*Tilia vulgaris*)   15, 65

M
McNamee, Jackie   92-5
materials *see* wood
maternity   92-4
medieval-style carving   102-5
Mould, Glyn   38-40
murals   37
mythology, inspirational source   79-83

N
naturalism   88-9
nature, inspirational source   12-16, 23
Neil, Geoff and Hedley   96-7
Nicoll, Judith   79-83

O
oak (*Quercus spp*)   66, 105
old wood   51

P
painting
    see also colouring
    large sculptures   94
    using acrylics   26
Panor, Uri   84-7
Pascoe, Peter   38-40
patinas, antique effect   52
Phillips, Ann and Bob   35-7
Pizzey, Graham   35-7
Placet, Suzy   20-3
playgrounds   76
Powell, Don   71-3
power tools   29-31
    see also chainsaws; saws
pricing   18, 40, 115-16
projects, site specific   63
purlins   102-5

Q
quotations *see* pricing

R
Rankin, Don   98-101
realism   88, 96-7
relief carving   10-11, 36, 107-8
religion   6-9
restoration   39, 105
Roberts, Trevor   64-7

S
saws, electric   93
Saylan, Ed   88-91
scale   7, 34
Schroeder, Roger   24-6, 50-4
sculpture
    large   7-9, 12-16, 20-3, 41-5, 61-3, 64-7
                 74-8, 92-5, 98-101, 110-13
    markets for   5
sealing
    carvings   83
    preparatory   28

selling   18-19, 114-15
    large sculptures   5
sharpening   37, 116
sheep   59
Siberia   84-7
sites, working on   110
small businesses   17-19
splits *see* cracks
straw   60
Styles, Adam   32-4
sycamore (*Acer pseudoplatanus*) 43

T
teak (*Tectona spp*)   36
techniques *see* working methods
tools
    see also gouges; power tools
    production   54
    second-hand   32
    selection   14, 16, 36, 116
        figure carving   48-9
        restoration work   39
        large sculptures   66, 76, 93
    sharpening   37, 116
Tudor-Craig, Pamela   9

U
unseasoned wood   65

V
Victorian carving   114-19
Vincent, Ted   12-16

W
war memorial   98-101
wellingtonia (*Sequoiadendron gigantium*) 43-5
Widmer, Charles   46-9
Wilbourn, Colin   110-13
Wolf, Madeleine   117-19
women, in sculpture   92-4
wood
    ageing   52
    burning   52, 75, 100
    colouring   65
    old   51
    sealing   28
    selection   29, 116
        figure carving   49, 73
        large sculptures   15, 21, 65-6
        relief carving   36
    storage   43
    supply   4, 27-8, 32-4
                                  49, 51, 116
        large sculptures   8, 41, 43, 61
                                  65, 92-3, 99
        restoration work   40
    unseasoned   65
working methods   4, 38, 53-4, 81-2, 88-91
    figure carving   47-8
    large sculptures   8, 9, 15-16, 41-5
                                  66, 76-8, 93-4
writing, using a soldering iron   60

Y
yew   58

TITLES AVAILABLE FROM
GMC Publications

◆

— BOOKS —

WOODTURNING

Adventures in Woodturning	*David Springett*	Practical Tips for Turners & Carvers	*GMC Publications*
Bert Marsh: Woodturner	*Bert Marsh*	Practical Tips for Woodturners	*GMC Publications*
Bill Jones' Notes from the Turning Shop	*Bill Jones*	Spindle Turning	*GMC Publications*
Carving on Turning	*Chris Pye*	Turning Miniatures in Wood	*John Sainsbury*
Colouring Techniques for Woodturners	*Jan Sanders*	Turning Wooden Toys	*Terry Lawrence*
Decorative Techniques for Woodturners	*Hilary Bowen*	Useful Woodturning Projects	*GMC Publications*
Faceplate Turning: Features, Projects, Practice	*GMC Publications*	Woodturning: A Foundation Course	*Keith Rowley*
Green Woodwork	*Mike Abbott*	Woodturning Jewellery	*Hilary Bowen*
Illustrated Woodturning Techniques	*John Hunnex*	Woodturning Masterclass	*Tony Boase*
Keith Rowley's Woodturning Projects	*Keith Rowley*	Woodturning: A Source Book of Shapes	*John Hunnex*
Make Money from Woodturning	*Ann & Bob Phillips*	Woodturning Techniques	*GMC Publications*
Multi-Centre Woodturning	*Ray Hopper*	Woodturning Wizardry	*David Springett*
Pleasure & Profit from Woodturning	*Reg Sherwin*		

WOODCARVING

The Art of the Woodcarver	*GMC Publications*	Wildfowl Carving Volume 1	*Jim Pearce*
Carving Birds & Beasts	*GMC Publications*	Wildfowl Carving Volume 2	*Jim Pearce*
Carving Realistic Birds	*David Tippey*	Woodcarving: A Complete Course	*Ron Butterfield*
Carving on Turning	*Chris Pye*	Woodcarving for Beginners:	
Decorative Woodcarving	*Jeremy Williams*	Projects, Techniques & Tools	*GMC Publications*
Practical Tips for Turners & Carvers	*GMC Publications*	Woodcarving Tools, Materials & Equipment	*Chris Pye*

PLANS, PROJECTS, TOOLS & THE WORKSHOP

40 More Woodworking Plans & Projects	*GMC Publications*	Sharpening Pocket Reference Book	*Jim Kingshott*
Electric Woodwork: Power Tool Woodworking	*Jeremy Broun*	Woodworking Plans & Projects	*GMC Publications*
The Incredible Router	*Jeremy Broun*	The Workshop	*Jim Kingshott*
Making & Modifying Woodworking Tools	*Jim Kingshott*		
Sharpening: The Complete Guide	*Jim Kingshott*		

TOYS & MINIATURES

Designing & Making Wooden Toys	*Terry Kelly*	Making Wooden Toys & Games	*Jeff & Jennie Loader*
Heraldic Miniature Knights	*Peter Greenhill*	Miniature Needlepoint Carpets	*Janet Granger*
Making Board, Peg & Dice Games	*Jeff & Jennie Loader*	Restoring Rocking Horses	*Clive Green & Anthony Dew*
Making Little Boxes from Wood	*John Bennett*	Turning Miniatures in Wood	*John Sainsbury*
Making Unusual Miniatures	*Graham Spalding*	Turning Wooden Toys	*Terry Lawrence*

CREATIVE CRAFTS

The Complete Pyrography	*Stephen Poole*	Making Knitwear Fit	*Pat Ashforth & Steve Plummer*
Cross Stitch on Colour	*Sheena Rogers*	Miniature Needlepoint Carpets	*Janet Granger*
Embroidery Tips & Hints	*Harold Hayes*	Tatting Collage: Adventurous Ideas for Tatters	*Lindsay Rogers*
Creating Knitwear Designs	*Pat Ashforth & Steve Plummer*		